THE SIMPLIFIED CRYPTOCURRENCY

(Understanding the basics and secrets of the market)

TOLA JOSEPH FADUGBAGBE

Copyright © 2021 Tola Joseph Fadugbagbe

All rights reserved. No part of this publication may be reproduced, distributed, or transmitted in any form or by any means, including photocopying, recording, or other electronic or mechanical method without the prior written permission of the publisher, except in the case of brief quotations embodied in critical reviews and certain other noncommercial uses permitted by copyright law. For permission requests, write to the publisher, addressed "Attention: Permissions Coordinator," at the address below.

Printed by:
Haybee Multimedia
123, Awolowo Avenue, Isale Igbein, Abeokuta, Ogun State.
+2347032633902

This book is © Tola Joseph Fadugbagbe. All Rights Reserved. You may not sell this book, give it away, display it in public, or may you distribute it in any form whatsoever.

We made reasonable attempts to ensure the information provided in this publication; the author does not assume any responsibility for errors, omissions, or contrary interpretation of this information and any damages or costs incurred.

The content of this book should not be used as a source of legal, business, accounting, or financial advice. All readers are advised to seek the services of competent professionals in legal, business, accounting, and finance fields. While past results may be used occasionally in this work, they are intended to be just for example.

No representation is made or implied that the reader will do as well by using any of the techniques mentioned in this book. The contents of this book are based solely on the author's personal experiences. The author does not assume any responsibility or liability for what you choose to do with this information. Use your judgment.

Any perceived slight of specific people or organizations and any resemblance to characters living, dead, or otherwise, actual or fictitious, is unintentional. You are encouraged to print this book for easy reading. However, you use this information at your own risk.

TABLE OF CONTENTS

Chapter One
Welcome To The World Of Cryptocurrency — 1

Chapter Two
History And Meaning Of Cryptocurrency — 14

Chapter Three
Cryptocurrency And The World Market — 31

Chapter Four
Why You Should Consider A Cryptocurrency Portfolio — 45

Chapter Five
The Difference Between Cryptocurrency And Other Classes Of Investment — 57

Chapter Six
Myths About Cryptocurrency — 71

Chapter Seven
How To Start Your Cryptocurrency Investment — 83

Chapter Eight
Secrets To Knowing The Right Cryptocurrency To Acquire — 95

Chapter Nine
Basic Trading Techniques — 107

Chapter Ten
Airdrop: The Hidden Goldmine In Cryptocurrency — 120

Chapter One

WELCOME TO THE WORLD OF CRYPTOCURRENCY

Cryptocurrency

Everyone desires to control their money themselves without relying on companies, banks, or governments and their fees and controls. That is what Cryptocurrency provides. As the name implies, cryptocurrency is a currency that you can use for exchange. "Crypto", as fondly called, is a digital, or we can say a virtual currency. It mainly depends on the block-chain network and is very safe as duplicating it is impossible compared to other major types of currencies. It has made the exchange very easy, and the world is moving towards cryptocurrency or digital currency instead of the usual currencies.

History of currencies

While I understand that you are anxious about getting to the nitty-gritty of becoming a successful crypto investor, we must take a look at the basics to fully understand the need for this lesson and how cryptocurrency came into place. Currency, also known as money, is one of life's essential entities. We all know that money is a basic need of life, and throughout the ages, we have seen that the shapes of money have changed, but the purpose is still the same. The currency or money took start from several objects to credit coins and bitcoins. Now we will discuss the variation of money throughout the ages briefly.

Items like cowrie shells as money

In the early days of man, there was no concept of paper or coin, instead, people used to do exchanges through different objects, one of which is cowrie. As of early 1200 B.C.E, people used it for money. People welcomed the use of shells as money worldwide, and one of the significant reasons for this was that all shells were approximately the same in size. Shells can be found in coastal areas of the sea where they are present in a more significant amount. The shell has many types that are used in other places for exchange. The shells that were used by Americans as money were known as wampum. In some areas, the shark's teeth were used as the currency of exchange, and the Fijians mainly preferred it.

Counterfeiting

After the use of shells gained ground worldwide, problems began for traders as they had significant losses due to lots of counterfeits shells in circulation. This became a concern for people around the world. The government had to put specific measures in place to protect the currency and avoid counterfeit shells. The British government punished many citizens over the use of counterfeits. In the 14th century, some counterfeiters were put to death. One of the techniques used to capture the forgeries was that the firm that was printing the money left behind some deficiencies in printing.

In contrast, the forgeries made the same money they were using for some time, due to which they came under the eyes of authorities, and then they were punished. As we all know, counterfeiters are also present in this present age in an immense number. In America, these groups seem to be working quite easily, as they have good relationships with politicians, who ensure their safety. The maximum punishment for counterfeiting in America is 20 years in jail, while in some African countries, including Nigeria, the punishment for counterfeiting banknotes is life imprisonment.

Coins

After the age of shells and items, people changed their attitudes, then the era of coins arrived. Lydia, presently known as Turkey, in the kingdom of Alyattes, between the period of 610-c - 570 B.C.E, invented the first coin. The coins they used as currency evolved with time. There was a time when the son of king Alyattes introduced silver and gold coins which the people used for ages. The usage of metal coins lasted till this present age, as many countries still have them as a currency.

Leather money

This type of money was introduced after the 6th century B.C.E., and the Roman people preferred it. France has also used this type of money, and in the era of Peter, the Great's (1682-1725 CE), Russian also used leather money. In addition, the skin of white stags was used widely for leather money in the kingdom of the Chinese emperor known as Wudi. But after some time, the trend changed, and people stopped using the money made from leather.

Paper money

As we all say, money is not easy to earn because it does not grow on trees, but this saying was wrong in the reign (997-1022 CE) of Chinese emperor Zhenzong. Paper money was introduced by the Chinese, which is still present in this modern age. After using paper money for some time in China, it spread to other parts of the world, and then, trading began. Paper money has played a vital role in introducing the banking system to the world.

Gold standards

The gold standards were introduced to overcome the worth of money, which was decreasing due to fiat money. If you look into the age the gold standard was announced, some amount of money was equal to some standard of gold, and because of this, reasonable confidence was recorded among the investors and traders, which was a good sign. However, this step had drawbacks as well as some countries were unable to isolate their economy from depression. This resulted into inflation in most countries of the world, which was a sign of worry for the developed countries.

Credit cards

You will be a little bit surprised that until 1950 no credit card was used in the world; the first credit card was founded after the foundation of the Diners Club. In 1959, the first plastic card was introduced by Americans. Until this time, the cards were simple, and there was no magnetic stripe on them which was made possible in the 1960s. You know this magnetic stripe includes all the information of an individual's account. The security system of credit cards was enhanced after 1990 when a chip was embedded in it that secured the user's data. Until 2007, no one could have a lot of money on the card, and it couldn't carry it, but in 2017 users were enabled to have $1 trillion in their credit card. So credit cards have revolutionised the world. People do not need to carry a large significant amount of money in their pockets; instead, they use cards that are very easy to carry and can be used in any country where the booth is present.

Welcome to cryptocurrency!
Before discussing cryptocurrency and its norms and regulations, you need to know about the history of money or currency. The currency has changed with time, and it is the need of time. Every person knows that nothing can be constant throughout, and the same is true with currency. We live in the modern age, and everything has been revolutionised in the past two decades. Before the 2000s, it wasn't easy to connect or send anything to someone living in another country. It usually took about a month or two to reach him because there were no fast or direct means of communication. However, the telephonic system was invented, and after that, smartphones came into the picture. The telephone has succeeded in connecting the world and making it a global village. The same is the case with the courier system, as gadgets are now sent to the person living in

another country in two or three days. One can therefore assume that technology has changed the world and has taken it by surprise. If these things are changing and bringing positivity towards life, why not currency?

Why not currency?
As you know, change is occurring in everything with time, and currency shouldn't be left behind. It is quite important to pay attention to currency, and new things should be tried for exchange and trade; cryptocurrency has been introduced in the market for this purpose. America and China are the two leading forces in the world market. According to 2020 world G.D.P. numbers, about 34% of the world G.D.P. comes from these two countries, at a very high number. However, America deals in dollars all over the world. At the same time, China has its currency known as Yuan; there is a big difference in the worth of both currencies. The American dollar has more worth than the Yuan, but China has more exports than America. This shows an imbalance in the trade, and to solve these issues, there should be one currency that can be used and traded worldwide.

In this era of e-living, almost everything is done online, and about 40% of the world's population is involved in online business and online transactions. For instance, if someone wants to transfer money from Pakistan to the U.S.A., there is a significant difference between the two currencies. It will be costly for developing countries like Pakistan to overcome these problems. Therefore, cryptocurrency is the need of today's world because the loss-win ratio can be significantly reduced.

Cryptocurrency was introduced in 2008 by Satoshi Nakamoto; **not really a popular name.** The proper use of this type of currency started in 2009. A new concept was also launched known as mining in which a person will buy some currency and keep it with himself, and due to the demand of the coin, its rates will increase with time, which will be beneficial for people in the later stages of life.

An Introduction to Crypto

Like ancient currencies, cryptocurrencies specify the price in units - for example, you'll be able to say, "I have a pair of .5 Bitcoin," even as you'd say, "I have $2.50." Due to their political independence and primarily impenetrable knowledge security, cryptocurrency users get pleasure from edges not on the market to users of ancient rescript currencies, like the U.S. dollar, and the money systems that those currencies support. For instance, a government could freeze or perhaps seize a checking account set in its jurisdiction, making it challenging to try a similar fund control in cryptocurrency — notwithstanding the holder may be a national or legal resident. Conversely, cryptocurrencies go with several risks and downsides, like illiquidity and price volatility, that don't affect several rescript currencies.

Types of Cryptocurrency
Bitcoin remains the foremost and worthiest blockchain-based cryptocurrency. However, today there are thousands of these clones or forks of Bitcoin, whereas, others are new currencies designed from scratch.

Bitcoin was created in 2009 by "Satoshi Nakamoto," a person or organization who goes by the pseudonym "Satoshi." According to the most recent figures, there were around 18.8 million bitcoins in circulation as of November 2021, with a total market cap of around $1.2 trillion. There will only ever be 21 million bitcoins, limiting inflation and manipulation. Solana, Lite coin, Ethereum, Cardano, and E.O.S. are some of the rival cryptocurrencies inspired by Bitcoin's success, known as "altcoins." By November 2021, the entire value of all cryptocurrencies in existence will be over $2.4 trillion, with Bitcoin accounting for over 42% of that total.

Cryptography
It would be best if you learned about cryptography to understand the concept of cryptocurrency. Cryptocurrencies secure their units of exchange through cryptographic protocols, which are incredibly complicated coding systems that encrypt sensitive data transfers. Cryptocurrency developers create these protocols using advanced mathematics and computer engineering principles, making it nearly impossible to breach them and thus replicate or counterfeit the protected coins. Unfortunately, these protocols also hide the identity of cryptocurrency users, making it harder to attribute transactions and financial flows to specific persons or organisations.

Block-chain Technology
Block-chain is an essential step for every new crypto investor like you to learn about. A block-chain has a finite length comprising a limited number of transactions that grow overtime to record a cryptocurrency's entire transaction history. Every node of the cryptocurrency's software network is the network

of decentralised server farms maintained by computer-savvy individuals or groups known as miners who continuously record and authenticate bitcoin transactions store identical copies of the block-chain. A cryptocurrency transaction isn't complete until it's uploaded to the block-chain, which happens in seconds. The transaction is usually irreversible after it is completed.

Why are cryptocurrencies important?
If you want to know why crypto is essential, you will have to go through the past decade as it has become one of the leading currencies in the world from the past decade as it has gained importance among the users and developed confidence in them. Moreover, it is essential because no medium, authority or governmental institutions like the banks are present, and the transaction can be done from user to user.

Why are there so many cryptocurrencies?
A large number of cryptocurrencies present in the existing market gives an idea that the crypto is a very open source and can be accessed by anyone. Whoever is willing to have its coin will have to work on the cryptocurrency's code and launch another currency. It

means that many copies are expected to take effect in the upcoming days.

Bitcoin is still one of the dominant cryptocurrencies in the market despite many competitors, but the trust in BTC is recognisable throughout the world. It has a market worth of $1 Trillion, and by September 2021, one BTC was equal to $60,000.

Conclusion

Cryptocurrency has taken effect globally from the past decade and has progressed very fast. However, the world of cryptocurrency can be easily understood, even as its transaction compared to others is very easy. The world is changing its attitude and moving towards cryptocurrency.

Chapter Two

HISTORY AND MEANING OF CRYPTOCURRENCY

History Of Cryptocurrency

Know the history of cryptocurrency before investing in it. The origins of this virtual money can be traced back to cryptographer, David Chaum. The American created the E-cash cryptography system in 1983. Twelve years later, he invented another system, Digi Cash, that used cryptography to keep commercial transactions private.

However, in 1998, the concept or phrase "cryptocurrency" was first coined. Later that year, Wei Dai began to contemplate developing a new payment system based on cryptographic technology characterised by decentralisation. From humble beginnings in 2008 to price peak in 2017, cryptocurrency has taken investors and the rest of the globe on a wild ride. It has risen, fallen, rallied, and then risen again in just over a decade. Cryptocurrency is based on economic ideas and market efficiency principles. It is an asset that is not owned by a single body, as it is secured, international, fungible, liquid, and has a finite supply for trading. Because of the high demand and near-constant supply, prices have risen disproportionately quickly and drawing additional investors. Some would argue that the tumultuous cryptocurrency voyage paved the way for the thousands of other cryptocurrencies now utilized for financial and investment purposes. This is how it was accomplished.

The first known attempt of cryptocurrency according to my personal research) occurred in the late 1980s in the Netherlands, which puts it at 25 years ago. Petrol stations in isolated places were plundered for cash in the middle of the night, and the owners were upset about putting their guards in danger. However, the petrol stations had to remain open overnight for the trucks to refuel. Someone had the brilliant notion of loading money into the newfangled smart-cards that were being tested at that time, and electronic cash was born. Truck drivers were handed these cards instead of money, making the stations less vulnerable to thievery. At the same time, Albert Heijn, the primary retailer, was pressuring banks to devise a means for customers to pay directly from their bank accounts, which became known as P.O.S., or point-of-sale.

David Chaum's research

For newbies like you, the David Chaum research is of great importance. David Chaum, an American cryptographer, had been researching what it would take to establish electronic money even before this. His beliefs on money and privacy led him to conclude that would need a token currency that looked like coins and paper bills to conduct secure trade, particularly the privacy feature of being able to pay someone hand-to-hand safely and have the transaction completed safely and privately. David Chaum devised the blinding formula in 1983, or 25 BBTC, an extension of the R.S.A. method, which is still used in web encryption. This allows a person to send a number to another person and have that number changed by the receiver. When the receiver deposits her "coin" into the bank, it has the mint's original signature, but it is not the same number as the one signed by the mint. Chaum's idea allowed the coin to be altered in an untraceable manner without compromising the mint's signature, rendering the mint or bank 'blind' to the transaction. David Chaum's decision to relocate to the Netherlands was influenced by all of this attention, as well as the Netherlands' historically frenetic attitude toward privacy. In the late 1980s, while working at C.W.I. in Amsterdam, a hotbed of cryptography and mathematics research, he founded Digi Cash. He built his Internet money invention, enlisting the help of many well-known names, including Stefan Brands, Niels Ferguson, Gary Howland, Marcel "BigMac" van der Peijl, Nick Szabo, and Bryce "Zooko" Wilcox-Ahearn. The development of blindfolded cash was remarkable, and it drew tremendous media attention. Unfortunately, David Chaum and his firm committed some errors and were sanctioned by the national bank (De Nederlandsche Bank or D.N.B.). They reached a confidential agreement in which Digi cash's e-cash product would exclusively be marketed to banks. This agreement set the corporation on a merry dance of trying to field viable digital cash through various institutions, finally leading to bankruptcy in 1998. Because of the media attention, David Chaum secured some fascinating transactions with Microsoft, Deutsche Bank, and others. Still, he was unable to take them to the next level. Microsoft offered Chaum $180 million to put Digi Cash on every Windows P.C. at one point. However, Chaum claimed insufficient funds, and the sale fell through, and Digi cash ran out of money.

American crisis in 2008
People did not make much money in the beginning. And they kept whatever they earned in their home for safekeeping. People required confidence that their money would be safe as they started making more money because their residences may be stolen into and

robbed. People began to deposit their money in several banks after realising the necessity for security. These banks began to entice customers by offering a variety of deposit schemes. Now I'm going to take you back to the 2008 financial crisis. In the United States, banks began to provide hazardous loans to people to attract new customers, and as a result, banks were forced to deal with substantial loan defaults. Many banks failed and filed for bankruptcy due to people's inability to repay the money. Banks used people's money to invest in numerous chances simultaneously as they gave out risky loans. Some of these investments failed, and the banks lost all of the funds that their customers had entrusted to them. As a result, numerous financial institutions died. As a result of the widespread bankruptcy, the American government attempted to preserve some financial institutions from failure by bailing them out, allowing them to resume normal operations. The money supplied by the government to the banks was then also the money of the people, who had paid taxes. Customers around the country were dissatisfied due to the American government's activities. Because the global economy is interrelated, the events in the United States had an impact on the rest of the world, putting the global economy to a halt. The financial crisis brought to light the issues with having your money held by a central authority.

Meaning of Cryptocurrency

You need to know the exact meaning of cryptocurrency. A cryptocurrency is a digital or virtual currency protected by encryption, making counterfeiting and double-spending practically impossible. Several cryptocurrencies are decentralised networks based on block-chain technology, a distributed ledger maintained by a network of computers. Cryptocurrencies are distinguished because they are not issued by a central authority, making them potentially impervious to government intervention or manipulation.

A cryptocurrency could be a sort of digital quality that is supported by a network that spans an extensive range of computers. They're ready to exist outside of the management of governments and central authorities as a result of their decentralised structure. The term "cryptocurrency" comes from the cryptography techniques that won't keep the network safe. Cryptocurrencies square measure systems that give secure payments online is denominated in terms of virtual "tokens". That square measure is depicted by ledger entries internal to the system. "Crypto" refers to the various cryptography algorithms and cryptanalytic techniques that safeguard these entries, like elliptical curve cryptography, public-private key pairs, and hashing functions.

Explanation
If you are unfamiliar with technology and finance, you may find the technology behind cryptocurrency alienating. To understand how bitcoin works, you must first comprehend the most basic concept of money. Barter was the original method of purchasing goods in ancient times, and it was later replaced by shells, shekels, and other similar items. For example, we can present value stored in a paper bill. Paper Bills are also a type of money known as "Fiat money," a form of currency backed by government regulation. Cryptocurrency is a money technology based on a crypto algorithm that the government does not back. Due to their lack of governmental backing, cryptocurrencies are difficult to use for tax collection. Unlike fiat money, cryptocurrencies such as bitcoin does not have an endless supply; it was created to eliminate the risk of inflation associated with fiat money. Bitcoin is restricted to a spending cap of

twenty-one million dollars. Regulations Must Be Set for Cryptocurrency vs. Fiat Money, For Better or Worse.

Types of cryptocurrencies

Suppose you are trying to invest in cryptocurrency, it is important to know about the versatile nature of this currency. All these will help you to understand the basics before delving into the crypto world. Cryptocurrency has many different usages, and every type has its functions; usually, they are used for transferring money and used as digital currency; they are used in a distributed system of people. Furthermore, coins other than bitcoins are given a unique name of altcoins or tokens, which are also widely used throughout the globe.

The tokens have different usage and are preferred for various things like utility tokens. One of the finest examples is the Storj token, which shares files throughout the circulated or separated system. The other type of utility coin which is also famous is Namecoin, and it provides network addresses for DNS (decentralised domain name system).

Before investing in any firm, you should have proper knowledge about it to have a better idea of it. We know that there are two major types of cryptocurrencies in the world:

1. Bitcoin (BTC)

According to Wikipedia, "Bitcoin is a decentralised digital currency, without a central bank or single administrator, that can be sent from user to user on the peer-to-peer bitcoin network without the need for intermediaries." It is a type of cryptocurrency independent of other systems and can only be exchanged from customers to customers and from peer to peer. It is a digital currency with no involvement from external sources; also, no middlemen are required in the process. The bitcoin rate is very high, and as of this period, 1 BTC is equal to 48,289 dollars.

2. Altcoin :

The word Altcoin is coined from two words which are "alternative" and "coin," to form "altcoin." An Altcoin is an alternative digital currency to Bitcoin. It refers to a group of cryptocurrencies, ultimately all the cryptocurrencies other than Bitcoin. They are alternative cryptocurrencies that were launched after Bitcoin's success. They generally project themselves as better replacements for Bitcoin. As of December 2021, there are said to be over 15,000 types of cryptocurrencies, according to the price-tracking website CoinMarketCap.

Altcoins come in various flavors and categories depending on their functionalities and consensus mechanisms. Here are some classes of Altcoins you might need to know;

Mining-based
Mining-based altcoins are mined into existence. Most mining-based altcoins use PoW, which generates new coins by solving challenging problems to create blocks. Examples of mining-based altcoins are Litecoin, Monero, and ZCash. Most of the top altcoins in early 2020 fell into the mining-based category. The alternative to mining-based altcoins is pre-mined and often part of an initial coin offering (I.C.O.). Such coins are not produced through an algorithm but are distributed before they are listed in cryptocurrency markets. One example of a pre-mined coin is Ripple's X.R.P.

Stable-coins
Cryptocurrency trading and use have been marked by volatility since launched. Stable coins aim to reduce

this overall volatility by pegging their value to a basket of goods, such as fiat currencies, precious metals, or other cryptocurrencies. The basket is meant to act as a reserve to redeem holders if the cryptocurrency fails or faces problems. Price fluctuations for stable coins are not suggested to exceed a narrow range.

Notable stable coins include Tether's USDT, MakerDAO's DAI, and the USD Coin (USDC).

Security Tokens

Security tokens are similar to securities traded in stock markets, except for digital provenance. Security tokens resemble traditional stocks, and they often promise equity in the form of ownership or a dividend payout to holders. The prospect of price appreciation for such tokens is a major draw for investors to put money into them.

Meme Coins

As their name implies, meme coins are inspired by a joke or a silly take on other well-known cryptocurrencies. They typically gain popularity in a short time, often hyped online by prominent crypto influencers and retail investors attempting to exploit short-term gains. For example, Tesla, Inc. (TSLA) C.E.O. and cryptocurrency enthusiast Elon Musk regularly posts cryptic tweets about leading meme coins Dogecoin (DOGEUSD) and Shiba Inu, which often substantially moves their prices. In October 2021, Shiba surged 91% in 24 hours after Musk tweeted a picture of his pet Floki, the Shiba Inu puppy, on a Tesla.6

Shit Coins

Dogecoin, which some people call an "altcoin" and others simply a shit coin, was famously started as a joke and was lost to near obscurity a few months ago until the internet's number one "crypto Karen," also known as Elon Musk, decided to make a big to-do about it. As a result, Doge is now worth around an astounding $50 billion, more than the value of the Ford Motor Company.

"Shitcoin" is the term given to cryptocurrency that is useless and has no value. These cryptos were created as copycats, i.e., currencies that have brought nothing new to the crypto space. They are often created without an actual business model or purpose in mind. Unlike Bitcoin or Ethereum, which came about with specific, defined objectives and innovative goals, shitcoins lack functionalities and direction. Shit coins are half legitimate and half not.

For this reason, they don't have the longevity of other coins. Many shitcoins are created to capitalize on people jumping on the crypto bandwagon without doing their research first. Their value is based on speculation and little else.

Utility Tokens

Utility tokens are used to provide services within a network. For example, they might be used to purchase services, pay network fees, or redeem rewards. Unlike security tokens, utility tokens do not pay dividends or part with an ownership stake. Filecoin, which is used to purchase storage space on a network, is an example of a utility token.

Ethereum has been said to be the most popular altcoin, and people use the full name (Ethereum) when talking about the broader block-chain network but Ether (ETH) to discuss the currency itself. Other top altcoins aside Ethereum (ETH) include Solana (S.O.L.), Polkadot (D.O.T.), Dogecoin (DOGE), Ripple (X.R.P.), Litecoin (L.T.C.), Shiba Inu (SHIB), SafeMoon (SAFEMOON), and many others.

Let's discuss a little about some examples of Altcoins

before we move to the next chapter.

a. Ethereum (ETH)

Ethereum is a type of bitcoin that provides a software platform that provides intelligent contracts or, we can also say, digital contacts and decentralized applications known as dApps. It is a platform that offers a stage to everyone regardless of state, religion, and caste. Another thing that can be noticed is that this platform is secured from frauds and forgeries.

b. Litecoin (L.T.C.)

Litecoin was introduced by an Ex google engineer known as Charlie Lee. This currency is the second to Bitcoin's or the silver coin after Bitcoin's gold; this currency took effect in the family of cryptocurrencies in 2011. Litecoin is not under any national or central federation; it is an independent network and is the same as Bitcoin in many ways; the global generation rate is also excellent.

c. Ripple (X.R.P.)

This cryptocurrency was invented in 2012, having a market cap of $39 billion and one ripple equal to $0.82. This type of currency has proven very effective in transactions from one country to another. It also offers payments in different currencies, which is also one of the plus points in my view. Ripple is a US-based technology company specialising in gross settlement systems, currency exchange, and remittance networks.

As a newbie, you should understand that the market cap and trust in Bitcoin are much higher than that of some altcoins classes, so people prefer Bitcoin over altcoin. However, the main point that makes altcoins unique from Bitcoin is that they are here in the market to resist the volatility found in the cryptocurrency.

Special Considerations

Blockchain technology, which is used to keep an online ledger of all transactions that have ever been conducted, thus providing a data structure for this ledger that is entirely secure and is shared and agreed upon by the entire network of an individual node or computer maintaining a copy of the catalog, is central to the appeal and functionality of Bitcoin and other cryptocurrencies. In addition, every new block must be validated by each node before being confirmed, making forging transaction histories nearly impossible.

Many specialists see block-chain technology as having serious potential for online selection and crowdfunding, and significant monetary establishments like JPMorgan Chase (J.P.M.) can lower dealing prices by streamlining the payment process. However, because cryptocurrencies are virtual and don't seem to be held on central info, a digital cryptocurrency balance is tired of losing or destroying a tough drive if a backup copy of the non-public key doesn't exist. Likewise, no central authority, government, or company has access to your funds or personal information.

Conclusion

A brief intro has been given about the history of cryptocurrency. Different researches were discussed; not leaving out how the cryptocurrency is printed and made secured.

Chapter Three

CRYPTOCURRENCY AND THE WORLD MARKET

Cryptocurrencies have grown into popularity due to the decentralised ideas they promote and the possibility of large returns. Still, their volatility remains strong, and these assets have a greater risk of loss than many conventional assets. For a student in this field or an investor, it is an essential thing for you to know. In 2017, for example, Bitcoin value soared from roughly $1,000 to over $19,000 before falling to around $3,000. Then, until the end of 2020, Bitcoin climbed again, reaching new heights of approximately $60,000 before plummeting below $30,000 in the summer of 2021.

Cryptocurrencies were spread widely due to doubtless immense gains; however, their volatility conjointly involves the chance of dramatic losses. Cryptocurrencies supply associate degrees easy to use, a digital difference to edit currencies. The unrelated nature of the market makes cryptocurrency a possible fence against risk, a kind of life-precious metal like gold.

Understanding Cryptocurrencies

Cryptocurrency is a digital or virtual currency that may be used as a type of payment. Cryptocurrencies use cryptography to safeguard and verify transactions and create new currency units, hence the "crypto" prefix (coins). Cryptography allows you to encode anything easy to decipher with a key but impossible to solve without one, which means coins are complex to make, but transactions are simple to verify.

Cryptocurrencies are, at their foundation, entries in an immutable, pseudo-anonymous database known as a "block-chain" that no one can alter (except under extreme circumstances when direct editing is made). Counterfeiting currencies is exceedingly difficult or impossible due to the block-chain, a public record checked by many distinct nodes. It also makes tracing specific transactions between anonymous user accounts or wallets easier.

Global Appeal

Cryptocurrencies are digital alternatives to fiat money that is simple to use. Although consumers in the United States and the European Union may consider cryptocurrencies a novelty, many countries have mismanaged indigenous currencies. Venezuela's autocratic administration, for example, has become known for its galloping inflation, which has resulted into deteriorating living conditions for millions of inhabitants who lack access to foreign currency.

The enormous variations in Bitcoin and

cryptocurrencies could seem hazardous to U.S. customers. Still, Venezuelans could notice the swings bearable given that their domestic currency has been in a sharp reduction for several years and shows no signs of decreasing. In other words, because the quantity of cryptocurrency coins in circulation is mathematically restricted over time, many worldwide consumers may consider cryptocurrencies as a hedge against inflation. Other governments impose stringent capital controls and levy substantial taxes to regulate the movement of money. However, cryptocurrencies can be used to avoid capital controls and taxes, whether legal or not, resulting in increasing demand from consumers and enterprises. As a result, many countries have begun to crack down on the illicit use of cryptocurrencies for tax evasion, as well as illegal purchases and transactions in other countries.

Government Responses

The official response to cryptocurrencies has been tepid at best across central banks and monetary establishments. Whereas some organizations are auxiliary, several significant banks stay cautious giving the market's extreme volatility. Moreover, problems with nonpayment and capital control even have semiconductor diode to some widespread issues.

United States Federal Reserve

According to U.S. Federal Reserve Chairman Jerome Powell, technical difficulties will remain, governance and risk management will be critical before cryptocurrencies become mainstream and enter the world market.

European Central Bank

Former European Central Bank Vice President Victor Constancio referred to Bitcoin as a "tulip" about the 17th-century Dutch bubble, and many other governors have expressed similar reservations. So they clearly are stating this as a good sign and wishing it could do better soon, but some of the officials are still concerned about the flow of cryptocurrency in the mainstream market.

People's Bank of China

The People's Bank of China believes that the time is "ripe" to welcome cryptocurrencies. Still, the central bank wants complete control, and officials are cracking down on the country's cryptocurrency sector. So they are clearly stating that they are ready enough to welcome the cryptocurrency industry. However, they are facing obstacles with backstabbing by some people.

Bank of Japan

At the immediate start of cryptocurrency, the Bank of Japan showed its concerns and talked about the transparency of crypto in the world market. Furthermore, they described it clearly that they do not see its future in the market.

Bank of England

Former Bank of England Governor, Mark Carney described cryptocurrencies as a "revolution" in finance, making the central bank one of the few government backers of the technology. So at that time when most of the people were criticising it, Bank of England was one of those who supported it well and welcomed it reasonably.

The Venezuelan Government

Faced with its funding constraints, the Venezuelan government developed its cryptocurrency, the "petro," in 2018, reportedly backed by crude oil barrels. While official sources claim that the government raised billions of cash, many analysts doubt these statistics, and the United States has banned Americans from acquiring cryptocurrencies.

Impact on Global Investments

Cryptocurrencies have many edges over the usual currency, involving resistance transactions and inflation management. However, several investors square measure adding these currencies to their heterogeneous portfolios. Particularly, the unrelated nature of the market makes cryptocurrencies a possible fence against risk; just like gold. Several cryptocurrency exchange-traded merchandise has arisen for this terrible reason.

On the opposite hand, some specialists worry that a cryptocurrency crash may harm the broader market, almost like mortgage-backed securities sparked a wider international money crisis, noting that the overall. Capitalisation of all cryptocurrencies, that is between one and 2 trillion bucks currently, continues to be but that of some massive public corporations, like Meta (formerly Facebook) or Amazon. In the end, several investors read cryptocurrencies as either a vehicle for speculation or a hedge against inflation; the market scale does not represent a general risk as of 2021.

Cryptocurrency And The African Market

Africa is the second-most-populous continent globally, with around 1.3 billion people. However, due to historical issues with colonialism, civil wars, and harsh terrains, African countries have suffered from infrastructure problems for a long time. This has made financial services less accessible, leading to around 57% of the population remaining unbanked.

At the same time, bad infrastructural development has made Africa a perfect vector for cryptocurrencies because people only need a smartphone to access blockchain networks. Tim Fries, Co-founder and editor of The Tokenist, described Nigeria as the vanguard of crypto adoption for the entire world.

Recently, the cryptocurrency trading market in Africa has grown drastically, reporting over $105 billion growth from July 2020 to mid-2021. In addition, several countries from the region ranked in the top 20 of the Global Crypto Adoption Index. This includes countries like South Africa and Kenya, among others.

The Economic Impact of Cryptocurrency

Since the start of Bitcoin in 2009, the implementation of the cryptocurrency has been apparent to the general public. The new type of currency has established itself as a preferred and viable currency supply across the planet due to its autonomy and convenient nature. Different types of cryptocurrency were unreal to function as an alternate currency supply.

As of January 2020, there were over 2000 cryptocurrencies that exist. Additionally, nearly 36.5 million within the North American country own or invest in some form of currency. Cryptocurrencies like Bitcoins are area units enjoyed due to the supply of an additional contemporary and digital-based form of currency. These sites don't utilize a 3rd party to move with transactions. This permits transactions to travel directly from purchaser to marketer. Bitcoin has also been applauded for its several advantages, such as low dealing fees and quicker process. That explains why there are many billions of bucks flowing into the new types of currency in recent years. Block-chain, the technology behind cryptocurrency, has finally taken a step towards the thought.

Cryptocurrency provides several incentives for entrepreneurs across the world. It has made it easier for entrepreneurs to succeed in international markets instead of being strictly protrusive to the national markets. This has allowed sellers to create relationships and foster trust with markets which was never before offered and has been fantastic for developing nations. Throughout the last 3 months of 2020, day by day saw a mean of 287 thousand confirmed Bitcoin transactions worldwide. However, this new currency style still has disadvantages that have prevented it from taking that next step. One of the main problems with online currency is the failure to shield patrons. As a result of the site's area unit being against employing a third party to delegate transactions, some patron's area units were left scammed. Like the Bitcoin area unit, currencies are solely accepted by a tiny cluster of online patrons. Cryptocurrency has provided brand new technology-based thanks to moving business. The market has led to several new patrons and allowed international trade to happen a lot of swimmingly. Even supposing the demand has increased, it has ways to travel before it takes that next leap to be a widely used sort of currency.

Cryptocurrency Market Size Forecast to 2026 with COVID-19 Impact Analysis

The COVID-19 pandemic has had an extensive impact on the worldwide financial system. With the virus spreading across 188 countries, various companies were packed up, and many folks lost their jobs. The virus primarily affected tiny businesses; however, massive firms also felt the impact. Apple briefly closed all of its stores outside China, and Bloomingdale's constantly did with its fifty-six locations. Against the scenery of the uncertainty raised by COVID-19, Bitcoin, Ethereum, and different digital currencies have garnered strong attention. Banks within the U.S. square measure making their block-chain-based systems and digital currencies to modify cryptocurrency payments between their customers. Also, in October 2020, PayPal proclaimed that its customers are going to be able to purchase, sell, and hold Bitcoin and cryptocurrencies victimisation their PayPal accounts, permitting customers to shop for things from the twenty-six million sellers United Nations agency settled for PayPal in 2021, PayPal is going to enable cryptocurrency to be used as a funding supply.

Cryptocurrency Market Outlook - 2030
The global cryptocurrency market was valued at $1.49 billion in 2020 and is projected to succeed at $4.94 billion by 2030, growing at a CAGR of twelve.8% from

2021 to 2030. Cryptocurrency is thought of as virtual currency. It is a currency style that exists digitally and has no central supply or control authority other than it using blockchain technology to attest to the transactions. Block-chain may be a sub-urbanised technology that unfolds across several computers that manage and record transactions. Moreover, it doesn't trust banks to verify the transactions; however, it is employed as a peer-to-peer system that modifies users to send and receive payments from any place within the world. An increase in operational potency and transparency in money payment systems, rise in demand for remittances in developing countries, increase in information security, and improved market cap area unit are the most important factors that drive the expansion of the worldwide cryptocurrency market. Moreover, high implementation value and lack of awareness of cryptocurrency among the oldsters in developing nations hamper the cryptocurrency market growth. What is more, an increase in demand for cryptocurrency among banks and money establishments and untapped potential on rising economies area unit expected to produce a good chance for the market enlargement throughout the forecast amount?

Competitive Analysis

The key players profiled within the market report area unit advanced small Devices INC., Bit Fury cluster restricted, B.T.L. cluster Ltd., Coin check INC., Intel Corporation, Ledger S.A.S., NVIDIA Corporation, Ripple, Xilinx Inc., and Xapo Holdings restricted. These key players have adopted varied methods, like product portfolio enlargement, mergers & acquisitions, agreements, geographical enlargement, and collaborations, to extend their penetration and strengthen their foothold within the cryptocurrency business.

Segment Overview

The cryptocurrency market is divided into providing, process, type, user, and region. By providing, it's fragmented into hardware and software packages. The hardware phase is divided into ASIC, GPU, FPGA, and others. The ASIC is more sequestered into full-custom ASIC, semi-custom ASIC, and programmable ASIC. The supported method is divided into mining and group action. By user, it's classified into mercantilism, retail and e-commerce, banking, and others. Finally, the market is viewed across North America, Europe, Asia-Pacific, and LAMEA.

Chapter Four

WHY YOU SHOULD CONSIDER A CRYPTOCURRENCY PORTFOLIO

You might have been an investor with many schemes and operations before reading my book, and yet you feel like "why do I need to have a cryptocurrency portfolio?". So in this chapter, I will be discussing elaborately what a cryptocurrency portfolio is and why you need to consider one in this age.

Portfolio

Before discussing the meaning and the benefits of a cryptocurrency portfolio, you might need to understand what a portfolio is. For those used to stocks and bonds, this should not be too much of a problem. A portfolio is a grouping of financial assets such as stocks, bonds, commodities, cash, cash equivalents, closed-end funds, and exchange-traded funds (ETFs). You will be able to judge anyone's progress and good management of different company levels from the portfolio of a particular company. Stocks, bonds, and cash are commonly the foundation of a portfolio. This isn't always the case, but it doesn't have to be. Real estate, art, and private investments are all examples of assets found in a portfolio.

Stocks and bonds are the foremost standard building blocks for a portfolio; however, you'll be able to diversify your holdings with different assets like realty, gold, paintings, and various art collectibles. In portfolio management, diversification may be a crucial plan.

Understanding Portfolios

Understanding portfolio is one of the important steps for you stepping into the world of business. Understanding diversification is an essential idea in portfolio management, which means avoiding putting all your eggs in one basket. Diversification is a risk management strategy that involves spreading investments among various financial instruments, industries, and other categories. Its goal is to increase profits by investing in various sectors that will react differently to the same occurrence. Diversification can be skilled in a variety of ways. Your long-term objectives, risk tolerance, and personality all play a role in deciding how to construct your portfolio.

Types of Portfolios

The following are the different types of portfolio

Hybrid portfolio

The hybrid portfolio approach diversifies across many categories. Building a hybrid portfolio requires taking stock positions as bonds, commodities, realty, and even art. Generally, a mixed portfolio entails comparatively mounted proportions of stocks, bonds, and various investments. This is often helpful because traditionally, stocks, bonds, and alternatives have exhibited good correlations with each other.

A Portfolio Investment

When you use a portfolio for investment functions, you expect that the stock, bond, or another monetary asset can earn a comeback or grow in price over time, or both. A portfolio investment is also either strategic, where you get monetary asset with the intention of holding onto those assets for a prolonged time, or tactical, where you actively buy and sell the asset hoping to realise short gains.

A Defensive, Equities-Focused Portfolio

A defensive portfolio would tend to target client staples that square measure grease-proof to downturns. Defensive stocks act in dangerous times as much as good times. Despite how difficult the economy is at a given time, firms that build a product that square measure essential to lifestyle can survive.

Cryptocurrency Portfolio

Now to the business of this Chapter, what exactly is now a cryptocurrency portfolio. Suppose you want to have a proper record of everything, including your transaction and exchanges, you should consider a cryptocurrency portfolio because a cryptocurrency portfolio is the software that keeps track of your online currency holdings. It allows you to keep track of the performance of each coin and gives you analytical tools. Many portfolio management systems feature live cryptocurrency exchange feeds and pricing updates. They may even notify you of significant market movements.

Explanation

A cryptocurrency portfolio is a list of all the coins and tokens you hold in cryptocurrency. It reflects the total amount of money you've put into all of the different sorts of cryptocurrencies. If you own ten distinct types of coins and tokens, for example, your portfolio will contain ten cryptocurrencies. The total value of all cryptocurrencies in your portfolio equals the full value of your portfolio.

Your portfolio will become increasingly diverse as you begin to invest in more cryptocurrencies. You may find it challenging to maintain track of all your investments at some point. It is worthwhile to download a portfolio tracker in this instance. These trackers, which can be an app or desktop software, allow you to examine the performance of all of your investments at a glance. You can make your portfolio as diverse as you want it to be. New investors, for example, may have a modest portfolio with only a few tokens. For trading reasons, more experienced investors can have a reasonably broad portfolio of various cryptocurrencies.

Why You Should consider cryptocurrency in your portfolio

According to several financial consultants, investors of all ages should suggest putting bitcoin to their portfolios, so if you are a newbie, you should also consider it seriously.

"Four years ago, maybe one out of every ten clients and prospects came in the door wanting to learn more about digital assets and cryptocurrency," said Douglas Boneparth, head of Bone Fide Wealth in New York, a business that specialises in millennials. "I believe it's closer to 50% today than it was four years ago."

So he said it very clearly in a vague manner that the ratio of investing in this portfolio is increasing day by day, starting from the first day the ratio was one in ten by now, the ratio has risen by 50%, and that's a positive sign which shows that in the future the investment would be massive and can look for a promising and prosperous future of clients.

If you are considering finance in cryptocurrencies, a monetary authority will assist you in finding the right balance for your portfolio. Some could also be ready to assist you in getting coins or finance in different bitcoin-related merchandise, like a bitcoin trust or exchange-traded fund.

With a potential consumer who has created heaps of cash on crypto, it is better to encourage him/her to use the earnings to execute massive goals which he/she has. That may be shopping for a house or paying off debt. For different shoppers, it is essential to examine cryptocurrencies as a long investment. Obviously, the additional volatile associate asset category, the longer the time-frame you wish, adding that several stocks within the S&P five hundred area unit even as volatile as bitcoin.

Regarding volatility, to be sure, cryptocurrencies area unit is volatile, which might be a barrier for each advisor and investor. It is very unsurprising that advisors see it as risky. It is eight times as volatile because of the S&P five hundred.

Of course, one of the most significant benefits of crypto investments is the growth potential. While most stocks can provide you with a reasonable return on investment over time, nothing compares to crypto.

New currencies come out all the time, and many see massive jumps in value. Even more stable options like Bitcoin and Ethereum grow at incredible rates, making it easy for beginners to make money.

While crypto is also "newer" on the scene than different investment choices, digital currencies are still gaining traction. Additional investors are allocating a proportion of their portfolio to crypto; nevertheless, most crypto investors are entirely self-taught. There are many reasons monetary advisors have, for the most part, unnoticed cryptocurrencies like Bitcoin and Ethereum to date. Jeff Rose, a long-time financial adviser and the founding father of Wealth Hacker, a well-liked YouTube channel, says he understands why most advisors are staying away, which is additionally advanced than some individuals assume.

First, it's a chop-chop dynamic landscape. And if the adviser isn't currently updated on the most recent data and techniques, a consumer might lose (or gain) a great deal of cash in a rapid. And since most money advisors spend most of their time finding out ancient investments like stocks, bonds, and annuities, in addition to making wealthy long-run plans for their purchasers, it's apprehensible they can't conjointly dedicate the maximum amount of time to following crypto markets.

Then there's the monetary facet. Though a shopper needed to apportion a proportion of their portfolio to Bitcoin, most investment corporations do not provide this selection. This implies the consultant would advocate a technique and then send their shopper to another platform to execute the group action.

This conjointly suggests that the consultant will not get paid. This last half lack of payment can be the most significant reason monetary advisors are not giving out all they about the digital currencies. Finding it irresistible or not; however, most advisors earn commissions on investments they sell. At the least, they make a proportion of the money you have endowed them. This additionally means that the adviser will not get paid; however, most advisors earn commissions on investments they sell.

The cryptocurrency market is abundant with coins and tokens seeking your attention to mark a number of your capital. As a capitalist, you will encounter perplexity over those assets to select in your portfolio. Whereas it is subjective and varies in line with individual risk craving and money desires, there is continually a balance that you simply can do to safeguard your investments with lower risk while maximising returns over the future. During this article, we tend to explore this market with knowledge from the past and a guide, you to create your portfolio with time.

Cryptocurrencies allow you to choose between investing in the short and long term. Dips and fluctuations will not affect your profit as much over the long term. However, profit growth also will not be as significant. On the other hand, while short-term investments allow you to bring in crazy returns on investment, the risk is often much higher. So whether you are in it for the long haul or the short term, the choice is yours.

Cryptocurrencies are a new breed of assets category that guarantees higher returns but with equally higher risk. They're growing in adoption worldwide and are currently at a stage where their advantage inclusion in each future safe portfolio is yours. Once you enter, you'll begin with a crypto issuance of up to twenty of overall portfolio and slowly maximise the investment with time. They will be counterbalanced by investments in fastened deposits, gold, property etc.

The most effective thing to know about crypto investment is the ability to put the capital you simply can afford to lose. By keeping the risk to a minimum, you are no worse off once volatility strikes you on the drawback.

As you enter the planet of cryptocurrencies, it's necessary to realise the data that may empower you to make your crypto portfolio. Bitcoin is the leading cryptocurrency with a forty-third share of the the total crypto market cap. That means the market direction continues to be heavily influenced by the worth actions of Bitcoin. The simplest thing to do is begin a crypto portfolio by administering a minimum of a share to Bitcoin, followed by a share in Ethereum, the number 2 crypto. Mathematically, the simplest portfolio for risk adjusted returns in future is calculable at seventy-fifth Bitcoin, twenty-fifth Ethereum. After some months of understanding how the highest two cryptocurrencies work, you'll be able to navigate to take a position in different high twenty coins (you can see the list at coinmarketcap.com). Over time and confidently, you'll be able to go outside the highest twenty and invest in coins with a 10x or 20x potential although the chance is highest among them.

Conclusion

Globally, their square measure regarding a hundred and twenty million investors in cryptocurrencies nowadays. Analysts expect this metric to grow 10 times more over 5 years, and hence, the general market will definitely grow within the long run. The most effective day to enter a footing in crypto is now as crypto is increasing day by day and is regularising day by day whenever it is completely legalised, its value would go up straight out of the way and hence investing it would impact all the consumers and investors, so if you invest in crptocurrency today, it will help you tomorrow.

Chapter Five

THE DIFFERENCE BETWEEN CRYPTOCURRENCY AND OTHER CLASSES OF INVESTMENT

Cryptocurrency:
For some of us who are into investments, you would have wondered what is special about cryptocurrency and how different it is from every kind of investment. Cryptocurrency is a digital or virtual currency protected by encryption, ensuring counterfeiting and double-spending practically impossible. Several cryptocurrencies are decentralised networks based on block-chain technology, a distributed ledger maintained by a network of computers. Cryptocurrencies are distinguished because they are not issued by a central authority, making them potentially impervious to government intervention or manipulation.

A cryptocurrency could be a sort of digital quality that is supported by a network that spans an extensive range of computers. They're ready to exist outside of the management of governments and central authorities as a result of their decentralised structure. The term "cryptocurrency" comes from the cryptography techniques that want to keep the network safe.

Other Investments:

Now to know about the good and bad investments, you should have a valid knowledge about other investments. Some of the investment types are as follow for you:

Stocks: Stocks are a sort of security that offers stockholders a portion of a company's ownership. Stocks are also known as "equities." Investors purchase Stocks for a variety of reasons. Here are a few examples:

When the stock price rises, this is known as capital appreciation.
Dividend payments are made when a firm distributes a portion of its profits to its stockholders.
The stock holders have the ability to vote on stock and exert influence over the company.

Companies issue stock to raise funds for a variety of reasons, including:
* Getting out of debt
* Introducing new products
* Adding new markets or areas to your business

Types of Stocks:

As you know about stocks from the above information, it becomes necessary to know about their types. Stocks are divided into two categories: ordinary stock and preferred stock. Owners of common stock are entitled to vote at shareholder meetings and to dividends.

Preferred investors typically do not have voting rights. Still, they get dividend payments ahead of common stockholders and prioritize common stockholders if the firm goes bankrupt and liquidates its assets.

The following are some of the several types of common and preferred stocks for you to gain some knowledge about it:

Earnings are enlarging at a higher rate than the market average in growth stocks. Investors buy them in the hopes of capital appreciation rather than dividends. A growth stock is likely to be a start-up technological company.

Shareholders are paid on a customary basis by income stocks. Investors purchase them for the income they generate. A well-established utility firm is likely to be a decent source of income.

Value stocks have a low price-to-earnings (P.E.) ratio, which means they are less expensive to purchase than companies with a higher P.E. ratio. Value stocks can be either growth or income companies, as their low P.E. ratio may indicate that they have fallen out of favour with investors for whatever reason. People buy value stocks hoping that the market will correct itself and the stock's price will rise.

Blue-chip stocks are investments in large, well-known corporations with a proven track record of success. Generally, they pay dividends.

Bonds

If you are a person who deals in payments other than cash, you will surely have some knowledge about bonds. A bond may be an invariable instrument representing a loan created by an Associate in Nursing capitalist to a recipient (typically a company or governmental). A bond can be thought of as Associate in Nursing I.O.U. Between the loaner and recipient that features the small print of the loan and its payments. Bonds are utilized by firms, municipalities, states, and sovereign governments to finance comes and operations. Homeowners of bonds are debt-holders, or creditors, of the institution.

Bond details embrace the tip date once the principal of the loan is paid to the bond owner and frequently adopt the terms for variable or mounted interest payments created by the recipient.

Issuance

Governments (at all levels) and companies ordinarily use bonds to borrow cash, and you will have to visit banks for that purpose. Governments must be compelled to fund roads, schools, dams, or alternative infrastructure. The sudden expense of war may additionally demand the requirement to boost funds. Similarly, companies can typically borrow to grow their business, shop for property and instrumentation, undertake profitable comes, for analysis and development, or rent workers. The matter that enormous organisations run into is that they usually would like much more cash than the typical bank.

Characteristics of Bonds

The following are the characteristics of bonds that are necessary for you to learn:

Face price is the cash quantity, while the bond is price at maturity; it's also the reference quantity, which the bond institution uses once shrewd interest payments. For instance, say, associate degree capitalist purchases a bond at a premium of $1,090, and another capitalist buys a constant bond later once it is mercantilism at a reduction for $980. Once the bond matures, each investor can receive the $1,000 face price of the bond. The coupon rate is the rate of interest the bond institution can pay on the face price of the bond expressed as a share. For instance, a five-hitter coupon rate implies that bondholders can receive five-hitter x $1000 face price = $50 per annum.

Coupon dates area unit the dates the bond institution can create interest payments. Payments may be created in any interval; however, the quality is period payments.

The date is that date when the bond can mature and the bond institution can pay the investor the face price of the bond. The issue value is the initial value that the bond institution sold the bond.

FOREX EXCHANGE

Forex can be a portmanteau of foreign currency and exchange. Exchange is the method of adjusting one currency into another for a spread of reasons, typically for commerce, trading, or tourism. From a 2019 triennial report from the Bank for International Settlements (a world bank for national central banks), the daily mercantilism volume for forex reached $6.6 trillion in April 2019.

The exchange market is wherever currencies square

measure listed. Currencies square measure is vital due to the permit of North American countries to buy products and services regionally and across borders. For example, if you're living within the USA and wish to shop for cheese from France, then either you or the corporate organisation you're getting the cheese from should pay the French for the cheese in euros (E.U.R.). The same goes for travelling. The traveller should exchange the euros for the native currency, the pound, at this rate.

FIXED DEPOSIT

A fixed deposit, also referred to as a CD, may be offered through banks. Once an investor places cash during a mounted warranty, the quantity of profit or interest paid on the investment is mounted. The speed will not increase or decrease at any time despite fluctuations in interest rates. The charge per unit offered by mounted deposits is sometimes set by prevailing low-risk market standards, like the London Inter-Bank Offered Rate (LIBOR) or Treasury rate.

Fixed deposits will have maturities from one week to 5 years. Mounted deposits cannot be ransomed early. In other words, cash cannot be withdrawn for any reason until the deposit's time duration has been invalid. The bank will charge an associate early withdrawal penalty or fee if money starts early.

PRECIOUS METALS

Gold and silver have been recognised as valuable metals and desired for a long time. Precious metals are considered a decent portfolio diversifier and hedge against inflation - however, gold, maybe the foremost well-known, of such metal, is not the only one out there for investors.

Silver, platinum, and Pd are all commodities that may be added to your precious metals portfolio, and every metal has its unique risks and opportunities.

In addition to owning physical metal, investors will gain access through the derivatives market, metal ETFs and mutual funds, and company stocks.

GOLD

Nothing in the world has the property of sturdiness. Even a young person like you can sometimes feel unwell, which indicates a lack of sturdiness. Still, gold is exclusive for its sturdiness (it does not rust or corrode), physical property, and ability to conduct heat and electricity. It has some industrial applications in medical specialty and physical science; however, we all know it chiefly as a base for jewelry and as a kind of currency.

The value of gold is decided by the market twenty-four hours each day, seven days per week. Gold trades preponderantly operate as sentiment; its value is lower with the laws of supply and demand. This can be due to the new mine provided, which is immensely outweighed by the sheer size of above-ground, hoarded gold. To place it merely, once hoarders want marketing, the worth drops. Once they need to shop for, a replacement provide is quickly absorbed, and gold costs are driven higher.

Cryptocurrency vs. Stocks

Let's begin our comparisons by discussing the distinction between cryptocurrency and also exchange. Each cryptocurrency and stocks have their sensible and dangerous days. However, stocks have an extended history that creates it more accessible for investors to predict the long run. Stocks face entirely different styles of risks and business and monetary, market volatility, government rules, among others. However, on the opposite hand, cryptocurrencies have a suburbanised area unit structure. They do not have a government or a bunch of individuals dominating it.

Cryptocurrency vs. Bonds

Bonds are a loan from someone to a corporation or a government. In different words, once an associate capitalist buys bonds, the corporate or government from wherever the bonds are bought is in debt to it person. The capitalist can get associate interest on quantity for an amount of your time once the corporate or the government can pay back the whole amount. The foremost risk with bonds is that if the corporate goes bankrupt, the capitalist can stop receiving interest payments and even the principal quantity.

Cryptocurrency vs. Forex

Forex, also referred to as interchange, typically attracts investment in foreign currencies. Cryptocurrency could be a globally accepted style of currency; additionally, the investors U.N. agency pick interchange also deals globally. However, here, the catch is the entirely different economic conditions of the countries. Investors will expect positive results from forex only if the country's economy is in a very sensitive state. Therefore, the capital gains for forex may be gauged solely on the idea of the economy of the various countries. This makes it hazardous in contrast to cryptocurrency.

Cryptocurrency vs. Fixed Deposits
Fixed deposits square measure supported by the government F.D.s square measure, sensible ones will have a long-run investment arranged, you have to be compelled to wait until maturity. However, those that exit their F.D.s before they mature would possibly further act and invest in cryptocurrency. At least, the market is volatile there, and other people will create fast choices. Folks will exit after recognising the market costs square measure while handling cryptocurrency. However, having foresaid that, no additional mining effort is needed for F.D.s. Cryptocurrencies have to be compelled to be strip-mined. They have investors' time and a focus. Whereas, for F.D.s, you will be able to forget the investment until it gets mature.

Although folks square measure a lot of comfy and tuned in to the standard investment plans, cryptocurrencies square measure new and might have their execs and cons. So, opt for showing wisdom.

Cryptocurrency vs. Precious Metals
We know in today's time, the most reason individuals take into account precious metals to take a position is to shop for jewellery and alternative such things. So, the market sentiment is the sole worth determiner of metals like gold and silver. Now, let's bring up the risks. The risks attached to investment in precious metals embody their mobility, import taxes, and last, however not least, there would be tight security. Conversely, cryptocurrencies would not like anyone to transfer them physically. Since it's all-digital, it makes it relatively easier for the capitalist.

Conclusion
Above all, I have discussed the other investments and how they are different from cryptocurrencies. For example, in cryptocurrency, the transaction is safe and does not have outside influence like others; the officials or governments influence other investments. So while in cryptocurrency, the trades and dealing are peers to peers, there is no risk of facing any scam. In contrast, in

other investments, we face a lot of different types of scams regardless of the influence of governments. So, in my opinion, cryptocurrency is better than other investments and has a vague future ahead.

Chapter Six

MYTHS ABOUT CRYPTOCURRENCY

Whenever there is anything new and valuable in the market and can change society, people develop a negative mindset towards it. You need to stay aware of those people. It happens in every era and every type of situation. Some decades ago, no one would have thought it would be so easy to reach the other end of the world via a mobile phone call. People will always develop ideologies about the things they do not understand, which is typical for humans. You shouldn't allow that to affect you.

When smartphones were launched, there were even more speculations that it was a waste of time and money, people would become lazy. People considered it useless for students at that time. We saw that the narrative changed during the pandemic, that students are availing themselves for the opportunities of taking regular classes through smartphones. So the thing I want to make clear is that every item faces criticism at the start as people are unaware of it and do not know its proper use.

The same is the case with crypto currency. There are many concepts among people regarding cryptocurrency. Naturally, there are speculations; some favour it while some are against it, but for you, before deciding, analysis is necessary. In the case of cryptocurrency, the Myths against it are more than the ones in favor of it. Some of the myths will be discussed below in detail and their consequences.

NEGATIVE MYTHS
Crypto currency is illegal:

I remembered speaking with a friend in the early days of my crypto trading, and I felt a little bit discouraged when he told me this until I did some researches again. One myth about crypto currency in the earlier stages was that it is illegal, which is not the fact, and you will also go with my opinion. It was considered illegal because it was a new thing in the world, and also, the concept was a new one. Some people believe that cryptocurrency has given hype to money laundering and has disturbed the world's financial system. This concept is somewhat correct but is also opposed in many sections. One of the statements from the People's Bank of China regarding the transaction of cryptocurrency is as follows:

"virtual currency derivative transactions are all illegal activities and are strictly prohibited."

There has been a strong statement against crypto currency from the side of RBI as they consider it a threat to the macroeconomic system. So there are no regulatory laws introduced for cryptocurrency and bitcoins. However, countries like China and Russia strictly oppose it in certain aspects.

Crypto currency is just another scam:
Cryptocurrency is considered a scam by many people and countries worldwide, but the central aspect is that they have not tried it. A cryptocurrency sometimes appears as a fiat currency, but it is very secure and cannot be counterfeited. So the currency is not a scam, but the investors and the people dealing in it can be scammers and can cause problems for the users. One of the scams that can take effect is that the scammer investors will insist you invest and pay in crypto currency for the right to include other individuals in the system. And they will force you to spend more and get more rewards in crypto, but that is not a reality, and all promises like this are fake and should not be taken seriously; otherwise, it will be a loss in the future. Now how will we know that a particular currency is legit? So before investing in any firm related to crypto currency, we should do proper investigation about it. From the following attributes, we can guess that the cryptocurrency is legit.

- Block chain-powered

- Solid business plan
- Efficient in solving real-life problems.

Crypto currency will not last long:
This was one of the dominant myths of all, as people believed. They used to lough in the beginning that this type of currency will have a short existence in the world and would disappear after some time. Maybe you also lie in the same category, and you are unsure about it. The people were against online use, and they were considering it unnecessary. Still, there are many speculations about the future of cryptocurrency as critics see it as a risky investment for every new individual. The best example is of professor Grundfest as he is against it. Still, he also thinks that such situations arrive in life that the solution cannot be anything else but cryptocurrency. One of the questions in people's minds was how long will Cryptocurrency endure in the world's economic system. Researchers stated it will last till at least 2140, as there will be no generation of Bitcoins, but the transaction blocks will be confirmed.

Crypto transactions are anonymous
Many people think that crypto transactions are anonymous and are unknown. But the researchers are of

the argument, as they have spent time digging into such a thing and know more than us, that cash is more anonymous than crypto currency. One good example is the recent crackdown in China against money launderers making illegal money by doing transactions through cryptocurrency. So they consider it safe for them as no one will know about it. Still, they were wrong as every type of transaction is recorded in crypto, which is also against that individual's main identity, so no one can escape from the radar of cryptocurrency if they have made any black money through crypto.

Lots of crypto currencies are counterfeit
A real cryptocurrency cannot be counterfeit. It will always be legit as it has gone through several processes before entering the market. The process of cryptography makes the crypto currency one of the most trusted ones as it cannot be double-used after that. The crypto that is counterfeit is not a cryptocurrency. Still, it is the copy of it, and many uneducated and simple people are misguided by the forgeries regarding it, so they invest in it and are deceived in the end. One of the most significant advantages is that electric vehicles of Tesla are launching such cars that can be bought through

cryptocurrency, which is a significant breakthrough for crypto and the trust shown by known companies towards it.

Cryptocurrency is cash of criminals

Crypto was also known as the currency of criminals at the start because people were unaware of it. So the criminals took advantage by using it for their wrong and unlawful activities. One of the main factors that crypto is considered criminals' money is the tragedy of black market silk road in 2013, where Bitcoin was the primary currency. After this, the governmental institutions were active and captured many people, but the impression has gone wrong to the world related to crypto. Recently in 2020, an inquiry was launched against an account because it is associated with the silk road market, and after the inquiry, the result was that about $1 billion were seized.

The IRS can't track income paid in crypto
Internal revenue service (IRS) is a governmental institution of the USA. The tax collection is recorded on the transactions like we can take the example of the federal board of revenue in Pakistan, which is also the same institution. So when cryptocurrency came into

being, a concept was developed that the IRS is unable to track cryptocurrency transactions, which can result in many illegal activities like money laundering and forgeries, etc. The idea was proven true in some places but was mainly wrong. Afterword's a group of intelligent and quick investigators was established. The individuals in that particular group were trained people who knew about cryptocurrency; they started a crackdown against those individuals who considered that their transactions were hidden and that no one would know about it. The pack leader sends them a brave message that "we will see you."

Crypto mining is terrible for the environment
It is considered a threat to the environment because mining is done larger, making it volatile. Recently when crypto rose to heights of success, then china launched a crackdown that lowered the prices of crypto by 40%. Volatility is known as the ups and downs in the investments that can happen in bank investments and crypto. Volatility is not a good sign for any type of investment as it can cause many problems for the investors and their trusts. Some investors or a group of investors are also involved in creating a volatile

environment for their excellent, and we have recently seen it in the case of cryptocurrency before the crackdown of china. There are many reasons why the cryptocurrency is volatile, and some of these reasons are as follow:

Decentralisation: It means that everyone can mine coins, which produces many unknown buyers.

Lack of Tether

Lack of Thereof

Limited oversight

Security issues

Controversy

Minimal insurance

Multi-step exit process

Struggle for widespread adoption

Crypto is all about speculative investment

Speculative investment means that if you only talk about something, again and again, there is no existence in reality. The concept developed about crypto at that time was that there is no investment related to crypto in this world. So it is just speculation and is not based on reality. I was about the same opinion that it is just a game and doesn't base on fact, but recently the growth of bitcoin or crypto has shown that it's something that should be taken seriously, and it is no joke. For example, the yearly facts and figures of crypto are one of the more extensive evidence of cryptocurrency investment; according to Bitcoin.com, the daily transaction done through bitcoin is worth $10 billion. This is huge, and crypto backs it by regularly increasing investors and showing trust on the platform.

POSITIVE MYTHS
Real money and can be used for payments

This is one of the facts of today's world that crypto has become a real currency, and people use it for transactions because they trust them. This is also one of the essential things for you to understand. Crypto currencies such as Bitcoin and Ethereum were designed to replace the traditional currencies and the traditional way of payments like debit cards, credit cards, bonds, etc. One of the main reasons was that it has a very professional way of payments. It cannot be used all over the world. Sometimes, the use of these types of cards and bonds is restricted, so there should be a way out for that which was seen in cryptocurrency.

One of the best examples can be from real life. A year

ago, a Pakistani PUBG team was involved in South Asia and global PUBG league, and the moderators or organizers of the Pakistan region were Indians. When the Pakistani team named I8 esports secured a good position in the leagues, their amount got stuck with Indians because there was no proper transaction process between India and Pakistan to be carried out. Their payments were due for a year. Then the solution that came through for transactions was crypto currency. As we all know, in this type of transaction, only peers are involved and independent of governmental institutions. The transactions were completed through Binance, and I8 esports received their award very respectfully.

Because of the quality insurance system of crypto, everyone's trust is building up on them. In China, they have started digital transactions instead of cash which is an achievement for crypto to gain importance from such a significant world stakeholder.

Crypto currency is a good investment
One of the best myths about cryptocurrency in harsh conditions was investors have to do nothing. They needed to invest money and wait for their reward, which

was increasing by more than a hundred percent every day. If a person has bought one Bitcoin in 2011 for $20, that particular coin worth is $40000, which is a tremendous amount.

Cryptocurrency will replace the dollar and make trading easier

This is an essential myth as people started to believe in crypto as the dollar had different prices in different areas, causing problems. Still, at the start of cryptocurrency, its price was the same all over, which was intended by the people as a positive change for the trading community.

Conclusion

The myths that are considered important for crypto currency are discussed above. There are many negative myths while very few positive, but cryptocurrency has blossomed throughout the years and has made valuable progress that is highly appreciable. It is a legal currency in which different transactions can be made.

Chapter Seven

HOW TO START YOUR CRYPTOCURRENCY INVESTMENT

How to Invest in Cryptocurrency

As a beginner, the first thing to know is how to invest. When Bitcoin originally appeared in 2009, it was seen as nothing more than a fascinating phenomenon. Although technicians and futurists could see cryptocurrency's future potential in general, it was not attracting much attention as an investment. As a result, many people have no idea how to invest in cryptocurrency or its true potential. However, as time has passed and hundreds of new cryptocurrencies have come and gone, Bitcoin has emerged as the currency's standard-bearer. Investors and speculators haven't overlooked this fact. As a result, some people are beginning to envision cryptocurrencies as a worldwide alternative currency that will eventually replace sovereign currencies like the dollar and the euro.

Nonetheless, the enhanced trading activity has generated a significant number of traders. They're betting that cryptocurrencies, particularly Bitcoin trading, will soar to the moon. Fundamentals are rarely taken seriously by speculators. They notice a quick and abrupt price increase in any asset, and it catches their attention.

What Are Cryptocurrencies and How Do They Work

Block chain technology underpins cryptocurrency. This is a cycle of material registration and transfer that is not under the authority of any unified force. Instead, it works as a block-chain platform of digital payments that are not affected by monetary authorities. If you don't want to go into a technological coma, there are lot of technical intricacies about blockchain technology that you should consider. But, in essence, it cuts out the intermediary such as a bank and allows buyers and sellers to do business directly with one another. This should also help reduce or perhaps eliminate transaction costs, which are a big part of what makes cryptocurrencies so appealing. Bitcoin is the most popular cryptocurrency, and its price is routinely watched in the major financial media, prompting the question, "Should you invest in Bitcoin?" However, there are hundreds of other cryptocurrencies, many of which have already come and gone.

Understand what you are investing in

Understand what you are investing in, just like you would with any other investment. While buying stocks, it's crucial to read the prospectus and adequately analyse the companies. Plan to do the same with every cryptocurrency, as there are thousands of them, each of which operates differently, and new ones are generated every day. For each trade, you must comprehend the investment case. Many cryptocurrencies are backed by nothing, involving neither tangible assets nor cash flow. For example, in the case of Bitcoin, investors depend entirely on somebody paying far more for an item than they spent. To put it differently, unlike equities, where a company's profits can increase and drive returns for you, many crypto assets must rely on the market becoming more optimistic and enthusiastic in favour of you to profit.

Ethereum, Doge coin, Cardano, and XRP are some of the most popular coins. Internet Computer, a newcomer, has also later appeared on the scene. So, before you invest, make sure you are aware of the potential gain and risk. Your financial investment may be worthless if an asset or cash flow does not back it.

The Main Attractions of Cryptocurrency

At the time, it appears that cryptocurrency's two main attractions are:

It is anonymous to hold and use, and it is subject to price fluctuations that can make it appear and feel like an investment. And for those who purchased bitcoin before the price explosion in 2017 or the most recent price spike in 2021, it was likely the most acceptable investment in many portfolios.

THINGS KEPT IN MIND

Following things should be kept in mind before investing:

Bear in mind that the past is no longer viable:

Many new investors mistake looking at the past and extrapolating to the future. Bitcoin was once worth pennies, but it is worth a lot more. The real question is, "Will that growth continues in the future, even if it is not at such a breakneck pace? "Investors are interested in what an asset will do in the future, not what it has done in the past. What factors will influence future returns? Traders who acquire a cryptocurrency today need tomorrow's gains, not yesterday's profits.

Volatility

Cryptocurrency values are about as volatile as any asset can be. They could be thrown out in a matter of seconds based on nothing more than a rumour that turns out to be false. That can be advantageous for knowledgeable investors who can quickly execute trades or have a firm understanding of the market's fundamentals, how it is trending, and where it might go. Unfortunately, it is a minefield for new investors who do not have these abilities – or the high-powered algorithms that direct these trades. Volatility is a game played by high-powered Wall Street traders competing with other wealthy investors. As a result, the volatility might quickly crush a novice investment. This is because volatility frightens traders, especially newbies. Meanwhile, other traders may enter the market and buy at a discount. In other words, whereas professional traders can "buy low and sell high," naive investors might "buy high and sell low."

Risk management

You must control your risk while trading any asset on a short-term basis, especially with volatile assets like cryptocurrencies. As a beginner trader, you will need to learn how to manage risk and build a strategy to help you avoid losing money. And this procedure differs from one person to the next:

A long-term investor's risk management may simply

consist of never selling, regardless of price. The investor's long-term mindset permits him to continue with the investment. A short-term trader's risk management strategy can include establishing rigorous standards for when to sell, such as when an investment has declined 10%. The trader then follows the guideline to the letter, ensuring that a minor loss does not turn into a crippling loss later.

New traders should consider setting aside a particular amount of trading capital and just spending a fraction of it first. Then, they will still have money in the reserve to trade with if a position goes against them. The bottom line is that if you do not have any money, you cannot trade. Keeping some money in reserve ensures that you will always have a bankroll to trade. Risk management is necessary, but it comes at an emotional cost. Selling a losing position stings, but it's something you will have to do from time to time if you want to avoid much worse losses later.

Don't invest more than you can afford to lose
Finally, you should avoid investing money you do not need in speculative assets. If you cannot afford to lose it all, you should not support it in risky investments like bitcoin or other market-based assets like stocks or

ETFs, for that matter. The money you will need in the next several years, whether it is for a down payment on a house or a major forthcoming purchase, should be stored in secure accounts, so it is there when you need it. And, if you are seeking a guaranteed return, paying off debt is your best bet. Whatever interest rate you pay on the debt, you are sure to earn (or save). There is no way you're going to get lost there.

Step by step guide

Following are the steps before starting investing in cryptocurrency:

Allocate Only a Small Percentage of Your Portfolio to Cryptocurrencies

You will need to select how much of your portfolio you want to put into bitcoin ahead of time. It can be tough to make a sensible judgement in light of recent developments, notably in the price of Bitcoin. All investing is governed by a mix of greed and fear, and considering the advances crypto has made in recent years, it may be challenging to keep the greed portion under control. Bitcoin should only make up a modest portion of your overall portfolio, whatever the case may be. It's entirely up to you how much you spend. However, investing more than 10% or even 5% of your income should be avoided.

Understand that cryptocurrency is not the same as stock when it comes to finances. It pays no interest or dividends, just like gold and silver investments. To the extent that cryptocurrency will be a good investment, its price must rise dramatically and stay there for an extended period. Cryptocurrencies were never intended to be used as investments. They are exchange mediums. They are often regarded as a viable alternative to national currencies such as the dollar, yen, and euro. They are expected to become a more efficient business model in the future, particularly over the internet. This is because, unlike sovereign currencies, its value is determined solely by the market. But, at least so far, cryptocurrencies have not fulfilled the role of a medium of exchange satisfactorily. Because only a few merchants accept them, most transactions are conducted between people.

Choose Your Cryptocurrency

One of the true complexities of cryptocurrencies is this. There are hundreds, not just one. There may be a thousand or more. The situation is further complicated because more are being added all the time. That has to be set against the fact that hundreds of cryptocurrencies have already come and gone. And cryptocurrency as a concept has only been around for approximately a decade.

Bitcoin is the most popular cryptocurrency right now. It is also the cryptocurrency that is attracting the most attention and money. Ethereum is a distant second, with Z cash, Dash, and Ripple rounding out the top five. Bitcoin appears to be the most trustworthy of all the cryptocurrencies accessible, owing to its dominant position. Bitcoin has practically become synonymous with the term "cryptocurrency." The connection is intriguing because some cryptocurrencies have performed even better while the media has been closely tracking Bitcoin's price activity. Because of Bitcoin's dominance, you should concentrate your cryptocurrency holdings on this coin. Other cryptocurrencies should be kept to a minimum in your portfolio. And if Bitcoin, as the leading cryptocurrency, is speculative, any other cryptocurrency you own should be considered considerably more so.

Choose a Platform to Buy Cryptocurrencies

One of the drawbacks of purchasing cryptocurrencies is that they are not available in all traditional banking institutions. Banks and financial brokerage businesses do not provide them. You'll be restricted to buying, holding, and selling cryptocurrencies on specialist cryptocurrency exchanges for the most part. Following are few platforms for buying cryptocurrencies:

Binance
Bitget
Okex
Kucoin
Mexc
Coinex
etc

Store Your Cryptocurrency

The most common way to store bitcoin is in a cryptocurrency wallet, either a hot or cold wallet. This is a challenging subject, especially given the many wallets available. However, we will strive to distill everything down to the essentials. A cryptocurrency wallet is a piece of software that contains your private and public keys, allowing you to connect to the block-chain where your bitcoin is stored. Wallets do not keep your cryptocurrency; instead, they will enable you to access it on the block-chain using your public key (the "cryptocurrency address" that the other party sees) and private key (known only to you). To execute a transaction, you must have both. Because they're used to unlock your bitcoin on the block-chain, they are termed "keys." Finally, make sure that any exchange or broker you choose is secure. Even if you legally control the assets, someone must secure them, and their security must be strict. Some traders invest in a crypto wallet to keep their coins offline and out of reach of hackers and others if they don't believe their cryptocurrency is securely secured.

Conclusion

Cryptocurrency is a speculative industry, and many savvy investors have chosen to invest elsewhere. However, the best advice for beginners who want to start trading cryptocurrency is to start small and only invest money you can afford to lose. You should be prepared for volatility no matter where or how you buy, sell, or store your cryptocurrency. Traditional investments are significantly more predictable than cryptocurrencies. And, like with any investment, keep in mind that what goes up can also go down.

Chapter Eight

SECRETS TO KNOWING THE RIGHT CRYPTOCURRENCY TO ACQUIRE

At the start of the cryptocurrency era, there were few types of cryptocurrencies, and the people also did not know much about cryptocurrencies and their uses. The first cryptocurrency was invented in 2009, known as Bitcoin in America, which was used to buy a cup of tea and even pay for haircuts; it used a cryptographic scheme of SHA-256. Bitcoin was free and worth just a penny at the start, but the first rise in the prices of cryptocurrencies came in 2010 when its worth raised to $0.09 per Bitcoin. The cost of 1 BTC was increased to 1 dollar in February 2011.

As we all know, there are many cryptocurrencies in the market. Still, before discussing which cryptocurrency is the best one to acquire, we will go through some top cryptocurrencies, their year of inventions, market cap, and price in Dollars.

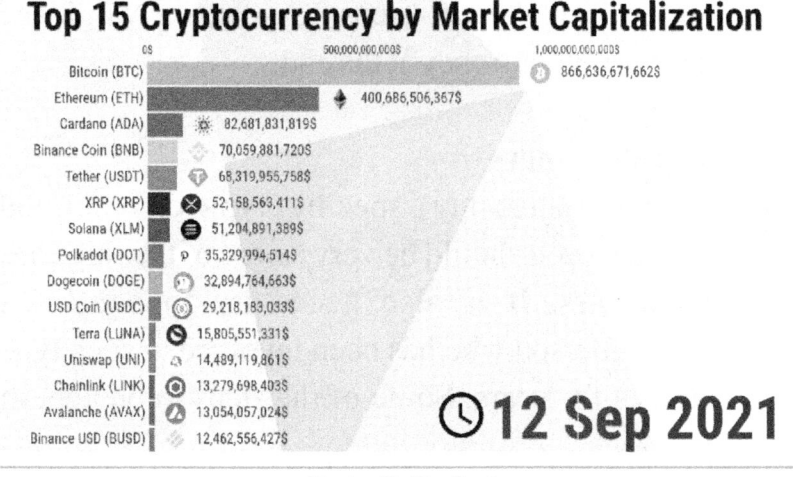

Top 15 Cryptocurrency by Market Capitalization

Cryptocurrency	Market Cap
Bitcoin (BTC)	866,636,671,662$
Ethereum (ETH)	400,686,506,367$
Cardano (ADA)	82,681,831,819$
Binance Coin (BNB)	70,059,881,720$
Tether (USDT)	68,319,955,758$
XRP (XRP)	52,158,563,411$
Solana (XLM)	51,204,891,389$
Polkadot (DOT)	35,329,994,514$
Dogecoin (DOGE)	32,894,764,563$
USD Coin (USDC)	29,218,183,033$
Terra (LUNA)	15,805,551,331$
Uniswap (UNI)	14,489,119,861$
Chainlink (LINK)	13,279,698,403$
Avalanche (AVAX)	13,054,057,024$
Binance USD (BUSD)	12,462,556,427$

12 Sep 2021

The above table illustrates some of the top-ranked cryptocurrencies in the world. For example, it is seen that the market cap of Bitcoin is the largest one in the world, and also the worth of 1 BTC is $47 thousand above, which is also one of the highest numbers. On the other hand, the market cap of Ethereum comes on the second spot having a market cap of $472 billion. These numbers show people's trust in these two cryptocurrencies that most people choose.

Now, as the crypto market is rising day by day and many types of currencies are stepping in the market, it has become challenging for every individual to judge which cryptocurrency is best and legit. Therefore, when a new user is planning to jump into the world of cryptocurrency, he should be 100% prepared for it. To be that much prepared, he should do research and go through many different steps to select a valid and profitable cryptocurrency at the end.

Steps for Beginners

Suppose you plan to buy a specific crypto currency and invest in it, so you should be very aware of the forgeries and fraudsters. It is also necessary to contact a trustworthy person who has been involved in such type of activities for years. Some of the steps to be kept in mind for beginners are as follow.

Invest limited amount
It should be the first rule in every type of investment that you are spending money on, so it should be started from the grassroots level. The same direction should be insured in cryptocurrency because it is volatile and can vary day by day. Besides that, there is no FDIC insurance for cryptocurrency, which is a disadvantage. Due to these negative things, cryptocurrency is considered risky compared to other currencies.

Although Bitcoin was launched a decade ago, people trust it throughout the world. However, precautionary steps should be taken before investing in it, and one of the most important things is to invest less in the beginning and if it works so then go ahead for higher investments.

Research thoroughly
Every individual who is planning to have a business or invest in something, does research before indulging in it, you should also do the same thing. When he finds a better opportunity in research, he tries to avail it, which

is the way to approach such situations. Spend as many days as you can in the study to know more about cryptocurrency and visit different communities and social functions related to cryptocurrency. Read articles related to cryptocurrency to learn about different types and values; it will help an individual make his mind to the right cryptocurrency.

Resist "Fear of missing out."
Before investment, every person should be confident enough to avoid the fear that they will miss out on any opportunity, and you should maintain the same qualities. There are many opportunities to look into and avail of those, and every person should be confident to invest and avail their desired goals. If you are enquiring about crypto currency and if something comes good to sight, it should be explored, and there should be no worries or fear of losing anything.

Don't trust, verify
Before investing in any firm, you should have a verification process before investing. Don't trust anyone too quickly because many scammers around these markets use different platforms. In addition, due to the higher use of social media, scammers have opted

for digital scamming strategies of which everyone should be aware.

Beware of 'Unit Bias'
Unit bias means that if you understand different types of cryptocurrencies like you can notice in the table so you will have the idea that different crypto currencies have different worth so if you are trying to invest, you should know about those fluctuating rates. Those variations are mainly because of the plate form of the currency, who is madding it, what type of utilities are used, etc. So before jumping into such a field, you should know about these things.

Buy a piece instead of whole
This statement is one of the necessary statements for you, and this is also related to the first rule for beginners. Suppose someone cannot buy a 1 full cryptocurrency so its not a thing to worry about because he can buy it in parts. Like we can take the example of Bitcoin, it is divided into eight parts or segments, and we all know the worth of a single bitcoin is very high, so if someone wants to invest in it so he can support the only worth of $10 in the beginning and can kick start his journey in this system.

Tax rules should be understood

Suppose you plan to invest in crypto currency and are currently living in the United States of America. In that case, you should know about crypto currency because in America, cryptocurrency is considered property instead of currency, so there are many tough rules for it. First, a person can suffer if he invests without knowledge in crypto in the USA. For example, in the USA, if you have invested $1 and receive a benefit of one dollar on it, you will have to pay tax if you buy anything with that amount. The second main important thing is that the annual record is forwarded to IRS. They investigate anonymous users and transactions, so you can face imprisonment for several years if you are found doing such activities.

Best to invest in

Above are some steps for the beginners to take while they are planning to invest in cryptocurrency, now we have to move towards another important part which is the best crypto currency for you to invest in. In my view, it mainly depends on the platform and the environment of a particular platform. Like we can take the example of Litecoin, Ethereum, and bitcoin, they are using a platform known as coin base. The voyager platform deals in Bitcoins. There are many other platforms like BlockFi, Uphold and Kraken, etc. Every platform has its advantages and disadvantages.

Before investing, you should be aware of the following things so that your investment is fruitful:

Community
If you are planning to invest and looking for a platform in cryptocurrency, you should first of all have a basic knowledge of communities related to different cryptocurrency platforms. Every platform has its community with different attributes and attitudes; if you interact with them, they are the best guide in every situation. YouTube should be consulted as well as different community programs should be attempted so that you have a lot of knowledge before investing in a particular firm if you need to know about the process and technology. Hence, the community is one of the finest ways out for that.

Fundamental Analysis
As you know, technology is increasing day by day, so before investment, you should have a technical analysis of a company or firm. These analysis can also be

referred to as fundamental analysis. The fundamental analysis deals with the ambitions, team, and strengths. Fundamental analysis allows you to select one of the best pieces from the market, like separating wheat from the chaff.

The Team

This is one of the major things to access as a new investor. Every firm has a separate team and works in a separate domain having different strengths. Now to know which team can bring you success in your investment, it should be analysed from the grassroots level to the benchmark. Like to see how the firms kick started and the different stages the team has been through. Some of the key features to know about the teams are:

How the team started working and who is behind it?
Do you have enough trust in their abilities?
Do they show enthusiasm towards their work?
Track record is heading high or low
Employees of the team increased or decreased.

The Technology

This is also an essential aspect as a beginner you should

have accurate information about the technology different firms are using. Moreover, you should know whether the technology in use will last long or not. For example, one of the best platforms is Ethereum because of its short contract. It is a technology that enables users to exchange anything of any value. This type of technology is the basic need of today's world.

The white paper
When you buy something, for example, medicines, when you open the box, there is an instructive paper in which all the things regarding the particular drugs are written like what it is made of, which ingredients are used, how to use and how to keep it, etc. The same is the case of white paper in cryptocurrency; everything is noted down in this paper, like how it was invented, then who initiated it, and how the progress is. So to know about a particular platform, its white paper can play a significant role in it. You will understand about all pros and cons of a specific platform from its white paper.

Their vision
When you were a young man under 10 years of age, you had some goals to be availed in the future, and that is your vision towards the end like if you have aimed to

become a pilot and now you are an engineer, so it illustrates that your vision was bigger enough. Bigger visions result in great ambition and success in the end. If you are planning to invest, so go through the visions of the firm if they have bigger visions, it therefore means that it is ideal for you. To also understand if they are working on their vision throughout or they have up and downs and due to that, they have sometimes slipped from their vision

Leadership

The main thing to know is that the leaders are confident and competent enough for their specific roles like CEO. Also, if leaders invest in a platform, it shows their trust in a particular firm.

Pricing history

The pricing history indicates the success rate of a particular platform as we all know that the highest price cap is of Bitcoin, followed by Ethereum. These successes in price caps indicate that these platforms are one of the trusted ones as people worldwide trust them. Of course, there can be ups and downs sometimes, but this doesn't mean that a platform is good or bad to decide about the best platform; average pricing criteria should be kept in mind and focused.

Road map

A road map, or we can also call it the planning of the future, is also one of the necessary things for you to understand. The road map tells you how they are standing in the present time, how many users they have, and in the future, what their target is regarding their users and price caps. This illustrates their vision and goals and how big and realistic they are. Therefore, every time you plan to invest, you should consider a more realistic platform that is more relevant in the real world.

Conclusion

From the above discussion, it is concluded that every aspect of a particular platform should be covered before investment. In my view, the two platforms that are beneficial enough for the investors are Bitcoin and Ethereum because of their track record, their market price cap, their leadership, and the number of users they have in the circuit.

Chapter Nine

BASIC TRADING TECHNIQUES

Trading techniques

A trading strategy is a predetermined finance plan that aims to generate a profit by going long or short in markets. Verifiability, quantification ability, consistency, and objectivity are the primary reasons a well-researched trading strategy is beneficial. Assets to trade, entry/exit locations, and money management rules must all be defined for each trading strategy. A potentially good technique can become unprofitable due to poor money management.

Fundamental or technical analyses, or both, are used to develop trading strategies. Back-testing, in which the process should follow the scientific method, and forward testing (often known as "paper trading"), in which they are tested in a simulated trading environment, are the most common verification methods.

Types of trading techniques

In a nutshell, a trading strategy is any set of instructions for trading a financial asset. However, the phrase is most commonly used in computer-assisted trading, where a trading strategy is implemented as a computer program for automated trading. For example, Mean-reversion and momentum methods are two types of technical tactics.

Long/short equity
A long/short strategy involves picking a universe of stocks and rating them based on a combined alpha factor. Then, every re balancing period, we long the top percentile and short the lowest percentile of securities based on the rankings.

Swing Trading Strategy
Swing traders purchase and sell as market volatility increases, and their trades are typically held for more than a day.

Scalping (Trading)
Scalping is a strategy that involves making dozens or hundreds of trades every day to profit from the bid/ask spread.

Trading the news
Long-term performance is the strategy of making a profit by trading financial assets (stocks, currencies, etc.) just in time and in line with the occurrence of events, and news is an essential talent for savvy portfolio management.

Executing strategies

A trader can execute a trading plan manually (discretionary trading) or automatically (automated trading). Discretionary trading necessitates a high level of expertise and discipline. It's all too easy for a trader to stray from the plan, which usually results in worse performance. In an automated trading strategy, trading formulas are wrapped into automated order and execution systems. Advanced computer simulation models, combined with digital access to international market data and analysis, provide traders with a unique competitive vantage point when employing a trading strategy. A trading strategy can automate your entire investing portfolio or just a portion of it. Computer trading algorithms can accommodate both conservative and aggressive trading approaches.

Cryptocurrency Trading

Investing in virtual currency price fluctuations via a CFD money market, or the sale and purchase of the constituent coins through an exchange, is termed cryptocurrency trading.

CFD investing is a sort of commodity that permits you to speculate on cryptocurrency price fluctuations without requiring that one acquires the underlying currencies. You can go long (buy) if you believe the value of a cryptocurrency will rise or short ('sell') if you believe the deal will fall. Both are tilted products, which indicates you only need a small deposit (known as margin) to have total exposure to the underlying commodity. Because the total size of your investment still determines your profit or loss, leverage will magnify both profits and losses.

Cryptocurrency trading techniques
Like stock and commodity trading, Crypto trading is riddled with dangers and hazards. Therefore, market participants must develop tactics that make trading interesting and safe to reap long-term gains from crypto trading. Let's begin by looking through several tactics that can assist you in achieving favourable results.

The following are some cryptocurrency trading techniques:

Day Trading
Professional traders engage in day trading, which is purchasing and selling on the same day. Positions are filled and closed on the same day, and no position is retained overnight.

Shopping for and mercantilism a security during a single commercialism day is thought to be day commercialism.

The interchange (forex) and stock markets area unit the foremost common, whereas it will happen in any market. The bulk of day trader's area unit knowledgeable and well-funded. They cash in of little worth swings in highly liquid stocks or currencies by mistreatment of high leverage and short-run commercialism. Day trader's area unit is keenly responsive to the factors that trigger short-run market fluctuations. Commercialism on the idea of reports could be a common strategy. Market psychological science and expectations influence regular economic statistics, business earnings, and interest rates. Once those expectations aren't met or surpassed, markets react with quick, massive changes, which might be useful to day traders.

Professional day traders or people who trade for a living instead of for fun, a square measure sometimes, are well-known within the business. They typically have a radical understanding of the market similarly. The subsequent square measures a number they want to be a flourishing day merchandiser.

Range trading

Two prices define a trading range: a support price and a resistance price, which tends to vary between them. The difference between the high and low prices in a specific trading period is the trading range. Prices keep inside a specific range throughout time, referred to as range-bound trading. To enter or quit a trading range, traders employ a variety of technical indicators such as volume and price activity.

Understanding

When a stock breaks through or falls below its trading range, it usually indicates that momentum is building (positive or negative). When the security price breaks above a trading range, it is called a breakout; when the price falls below a trading range, it is called a breakdown. Breakouts and breakdowns are usually more dependable when accompanied by a significant volume, which indicates that traders and investors are actively participating. Many investors consider how long a trading range has been in existence. Large trending moves frequently follow extensive range-bound periods. The trading range of the first half-hour of the trading session is widely used as a reference point for intraday tactics by day traders. For example, A trader might buy a stock if it breaks over its initial trading range.

Scalping

Scalping could be a commercialism vogue that focuses on profiting from minor value changes and creating a quick profit from reselling. Scalping needs a merchandiser to own a strict exit strategy due to one massive loss that might eliminate the various little gains the merchandiser worked to get. Having the correct tools such as a live feed, a direct-access broker, and the stamina to put several trades is needed for this strategy to succeed. A prospering stock speculator can have a far higher magnitude relation of winning trades versus losing ones, whereas keeping profits roughly equal or slightly larger than losses. A pure speculator can create a variety of trades every day, perhaps within a whole bunch.

The concept behind scalping is that most stocks will finish the first stage of a trend. But it's unclear where things will go from there. Some stocks stop rising after that initial stage, while others continue to rise. A discounter's goal is to benefit from as many minor transactions as possible. The "let your profits run" approach, on the other hand, aims to maximise good trading results by expanding the size of winning trades. By increasing the number of winners while compromising the size of the victories, this technique accomplishes outcomes. It is fairly uncommon for traders with a more extended period to generate good effects despite winning only 50% of their trades, or even less–the difference is that the wins are far more significant than the losses. On the other hand, a successful stock scalper will have a significantly higher winning trade ratio than losing trades, with earnings nearly equal to or slightly larger than losses.

Premises of scalping
- Reduced exposure reduces risk: A brief exposure to the market reduces the chances of encountering an adverse event.
- It's easier to get smaller moves: There must be a greater supply and demand imbalance to justify larger price adjustments. It is, for example, easier for a stock to move $0.01 than it is to move $1.
- The frequency of smaller shifts is higher than the frequency ranges of larger ones: Even in fairly quiet markets, a scalper can gain from several small alterations.

High-Frequency Trading (HFT)

High-frequency commercialism, conjointly referred to as HFT, might be a technique of commercialism that uses powerful pc programs to interact an outsized range of orders in fractions of a second. It uses advanced algorithms to research multiple markets and execute orders supported market conditions. Typically, the traders with the quicker execution speeds are a lot of profitable than traders with slower execution speeds. In addition to the high speed of orders, HFT is additionally characterised by high turnover rates and order-to-trade ratios. A number of the known HFT corporations embrace Tower analysis, stronghold LLC, and Virtual money.

Dollar-Cost Averaging

It's advisable to consider that timing the market is close to impossible when identifying the optimum entry and exit points in a crypto market. So, 'Dollar Cost Averaging' is an excellent way to go about investing in crypto (DCA). DCA is a term that refers to investing a set amount at regular intervals. This strategy allows investors to skip the time-consuming effort of market timing and create long-term wealth.

On the other hand, exit strategy could be difficult in the DCA approach. It necessitates a thorough examination of market trends and a grasp of the market cycle. Reading technical charts can also assist you in determining when to exit. Before making a decision, crypto investors should watch the oversold and overbought zones.

Arbitrage

Arbitrage is a trading method in which a trader purchases cryptocurrency in one market and sells it in another. The variance between the selling and buying prices is known as the spread. As a result, traders may book profit due to the differential in liquidity and trading volume. To take advantage of this opportunity, you'll need to register accounts on exchanges that have a significant price difference for the cryptocurrency you're trading.

Primary Research

Primary research is one of the most significant trading tactics. To perform a preliminary study on the worth of the item you desire to purchase, you do not need to be a trading expert. This entails keeping up with all of the latest developments in the crypto business. WazirX makes this easier by compiling all of the news stories you need to read before starting your day.

Furthermore, before betting on a risky asset class like crypto, you should assess your funds and define an investing goal.

Conclusion

You should keep in mind that Cryptocurrency trading is still in its infancy. While certain countries encourage cryptocurrency trading, others remain sceptical. In addition, central banks worldwide are working on better ways to control digital currencies, making crypto trading a risky proposition. There are, however, measures that can assist investors in avoiding severe volatility.

Building a well-balanced cryptocurrency portfolio that includes Bitcoin, Dogecoin, and Ethereum could help you beat volatility. Furthermore, investors can invest a set amount of money in various crypto every month. This will increase your risk appetite methodically, allowing your portfolio to provide favorable long-term returns.

One of the most common mistakes new investors make is relying on social media for cryptocurrency news. Social media buzz should never be used to make investment decisions. Because digital currency is such a trendy topic, misleading information about it spreads quickly. One should be well aware of all these basic trading techniques and crypto techniques, especially for the beginner investors and the old ones so that their investment doesn't go in a loss.

Chapter Ten

AIRDROP: THE HIDDEN GOLDMINE IN CRYPTOCURRENCY

This Chapter will open your eyes to a different thing we have not mentioned in any of the chapters, so you have to carefully study it as it is one goldmine you will need to harness in the crypto space. The CoinMarketCap has over 9,000 listed coins, which means that new cryptocurrency projects looking to attract investors and supporters will need to adopt some very creative methods to make themselves exceptionally distinguished from these other 9,000 projects out there. While crypto developers must promote their token projects extensively via social media, press releases, and crypto blogs, different marketing methods are also explored.

Once touted as an unconventional form of guerrilla marketing, airdrops have exploded in popularity since 2017 in the crypto space, with numerous projects leveraging on the strategy to encourage the community to help promote a project or as a means of rewarding loyal users. Additionally, an airdrop may also come from a hard fork, such as when Bitcoin holders received a 1:1 airdrop of Bitcoin Cashback in 2017.

What is Airdrop?

Airdrop is a common phenomenon for most people involved in cryptocurrency or is delving into it. While some see it as dangerous or risky, the simple truth is that Airdrop could be beneficial if only you can understand its concepts. It is one of the hidden goldmine in cryptocurrency if you know how to harness it. The concept of an airdrop is quite simple. It involves a business or brand "dropping" small amounts of free crypto en mass to individual wallets. An airdrop is a distribution of a cryptocurrency token or coin, usually for free, to numerous wallet addresses. Airdrops are primarily implemented to gain attention and new followers, resulting in a larger user base and a wider disbursement of coins.

The cryptocurrency airdrop is a marketing strategy for startups applying it in the cryptocurrency community. In this technology, the Bitcoin or other coins are transferred into some other accounts free of cost or in return for some small investments. The main focus of crypto airdrop is to make people aware of digital currency like crypto so that they turn their faces towards this digital world and proceed in it for a long time.

News of an upcoming airdrop is usually posted on a crypto project's website or Medium page, or third-party airdrop tracker and shared across social media platforms where many cryptocurrency enthusiasts can see. An airdrop involves small amounts of newly-minted cryptocurrencies and targets members of a select block-chain platform. For example, cryptocurrency startups may airdrop coins to NEO, Ethereum or the Bitcoin network wallet holders.

Benefitting from an airdrop usually involves registering through a google form, a Telegram bot, or directly on a project's website. Often an airdrop campaign will also offer the chance to get additional tokens for referring others via a unique link. The referral system creates an incentive to share the airdrop with as many people as possible. In addition, many people hear about airdrops through individuals sharing their links on social media.

A sub-type of airdrop is also referred to as a holder. The "holders" airdrop is when a token is airdropped to wallets that already hold another type of token or coin. For example, there was recently an airdrop of the Ontology token to holders of NEO. Holders' airdrops are typically not something you have to register for. Instead, they take a snapshot of a block-chain to see which wallets are holding what tokens.

Other "Free Crypto" Tools to Use

Of course, airdrops and crypto faucets are not the only way to get free crypto. For example, you can simply hold certain coins like ONT and NEO to claim free native gas tokens such as ONG and GAS at specific intervals. You can also employ DeFi techniques such as staking crypto or yield farming to earn digital asset incentives in the form of network rewards or new governance tokens.

When joining new exchanges, you can consider looking at various sites that offer crypto referral codes and sign-up bonuses. However, while all these reward tools give you "free" funds, they require initially investing and owning certain assets or making a first deposit to a centralized exchange or trading app.

Then again, if you are going to invest your hard-earned money into crypto, these tools can significantly help improve or even double the value of your initial investment, risk-free.

Remember, once the initial investment value has doubled, you can essentially sell 50% and keep the remaining 50% as a risk-free "freeroll" to use poker parlance.

3 Lucrative Crypto Airdrops Examples

To know how much of a goldmine the airdrops can be, we need to look at a few that have been very lucrative over the years. So here are a few examples of crypto airdrops you should know.

Uniswap (UNI) Airdrop

In 2020, Uniswap, the world's most popular decentralized exchange (DEX), airdropped its native asset, UNI, to all wallets that had used its platform and performed at least one transaction before Sept. 1, 2020. An eligible account received 400 units of the base asset. Unfortunately, most recipients quickly dumped their airdropped token during the event, and UNI changed hands at $2-$4.

Those who "held on for dear life" (HODL) were richly rewarded for their patience and loyalty as the exchange token's value soared with others in the DeFi ecosystem, climbing from $2 to a current $30 as of April 2021. As such, those of you with hands of steel are now sitting on a nice little nest egg of $12,000 from UNI alone.

Ontology (ONT) Airdrop

In 2018, Ontology airdropped its native cryptocurrency, ONT, to NEO investors as well as 1,000 ONT for people who simply signed up for its newsletter. In part, the event wanted to reward NEO blockchain users for supporting it during its fundraising. The total amount of airdropped coins was 10 million, worth approximately $42 million and trading at $4.2 per coin at the time. The token later shot up to nearly $11 amid a deepening bear market no less, bringing the airdropped coins to a valuation of $100 million. Sadly, that was the peak time to sell kids. ONT has since retraced to a more modest value and currently sits just shy of $2.

1inch Airdrop

In December 2020, the 1inch DEX airdropped 90 million 1INCH tokens to more than 55,000 addresses. An address needed to have traded at least $20 or made four trades before the airdrop day to be eligible. At launch, the price of 1INCH was about $2.7. Fast forward to April 2021, and the coin trades at slightly above $6.

One particular address received a crazy 10 million tokens (9,749,686) during the date of the airdrop as a reward for its support. That stash is presently worth $60.4 million in April, an increase of approximately $33 million in less than five months.

5 Reasons Why Crypto Projects Do Airdrops

By now, if you have read through the chapters of this book, you should understand that crypto coins do not just come into existence but with a particular vision and objective. Crypto projects give out generous bounties through airdrops because they are the biggest beneficiaries of such events. Let us explore the fundamental reasons why crypto startups conduct airdrop programs.

Creating Awareness

Spreading awareness is the primary reason why blockchain startups conduct airdrops. In the early days of crowdfunding, ICOs took center stage. However, problems soon arose. A flood of startups emerged during this gold rush, often with only a flimsy and partially plagiarised white paper in hand, oversaturating the market and jading investors.

Also, countries like China outright banned ICOs, and regulators like the SEC began to target ICOs dealing with domestic U.S. investors. Soon, new projects needed a more alluring and legal method to create hype.

The answer was simple. Just hand out free coins. The popularity of airdrops led many crypto supporters to go on a shilling spree, promoting projects to get airdrops and "pump their bags." Anyone active on social media's crypto scene can probably agree that airdrop recipients are some of the most vocal advocates a project can hope for. It was a match made in heaven for crypto startups since it allowed them to grow their community organically by simply shelling out a small portion of their tokens.

Rewarding Users

Many investors in the crypto ecosystem are only out for the highest return on investment (ROI) and do not care about a project's long-term sustainability. Therefore, they hop from one project to another, dumping their heavy bags after a pump and making huge profits off the back of small-time investors without providing any actual value to the protocol. Unfortunately, this type of behavior can damage a crypto platform.

To counter this, some startups conduct airdrops to distribute free coins to reward loyal users who use their platforms or hold a specific amount of tokens in their wallets for certain periods.

Decentralizing Token Distribution

Deep-pocketed investors may take advantage of their disparate wealth and secure bargain prices during a coin's early days, allowing them to hoard a significant amount of its circulating supply. The problem is that large amounts of coins in the hands of a few create centralization, which is currently one of Dogecoin's main drawbacks. In such cases, projects can conduct airdrops to balance out a token's distribution.

Attracting Investments

Crypto airdrops are followed by token offerings in most cases, whether they be ICOs, IEOs, IDOs, etc. A clever way to boost the funds raised without spending too much on marketing is through airdrops, as this strategy is tied to creating awareness.

When a project launches and conducts an airdrop, the generated buzz, if successful, helps drive the price of a token upwards as most recipients would shill projects that give them free money. Especially in today's online economy, where every interaction metric can be measured and used to attract investors, such as trending Google search terms, social media brand mentions, and community followership count on Twitter and Telegram, big investors or "whales" use these analytics as an investment weather vane to gauge a project's prospects. Therefore, an airdrop, which significantly increases community engagement, could seriously boost the company's overall capital for only a proportionally small amount of tokens allocated to the airdrop.

Learning More About Its Community

As a bonus, airdrops allow projects to collect data from the crypto community since some require recipients to fill a form providing personal details such as email, social media, and their views on crypto projects. With this information, a project's team can make targeted marketing campaigns.

Why is Airdrop Important or Necessary?
Airdrops aim to take advantage of network effect by engaging existing holders of a particular blockchain-based currency, such as Bitcoin or Ethereum, in their currency or project.

There are two main reasons blockchain startups and other projects would hold an airdrop. The first is to generate publicity for an upcoming ICO or token sale. Airdrops are often the first phase of a more extensive marketing campaign. They can be useful in generating initial buzz around a project. The referral bonuses also motivate people to spread the word, generating more low-cost advertising. Secondly, an airdrop is an excellent way to build a community around a project, even if not holding an ICO. I've seen many community-based, and non-profit crypto projects use the airdrop model as a way of building awareness of their goals.

Initial coin offering (ICO) is one of its known features. However, if you want to avail yourself of the opportunity of free coins, you should have a minimum amount of coins in the account, or if you don't have so not worry; there is an alternative method for that. You will have to promote the cryptocurrency on social media websites like Facebook, LinkedIn, Twitter, etc., or you can also write an article on cryptocurrency and its advantages. If you perform these tasks, then surely, in reward, you will receive the free coins or tokens.

It is very important for you to understand what crypto airdrop is and how it works, so as explained above, it is a platform that gives free Bitcoins or other types of tokens purely for their promotion. So shortly, we can say that crypto airdrop is a platform used for virtual currency promotion or advertising.

Good or Bad

There has been a discussion on crypto airdrop that it can be good and have harmful effects. In my opinion, it is a good and win-win situation for both stakeholders: the company and the users. Because users receive some free credits for really not doing anything special while the company improves their user population, which works in the company's favor later on. Many known people argued and presented their statements regarding crypto airdrop like Michael J. Casey, chairman of the coin disk advisory board, said that there is no other way than promotions to spread the cryptocurrency worldwide. His words specifically were, "the currency will not be considered valuable if it is not used widely throughout the world. For that purpose, money should be spent to gain the individuals". People have also been warned sometimes of using the crypto airdrop like Pierre Rochard, the founder of Bitcoin advisory, said in his tweet that "the crypto airdrop can be a flop scheme by the owners as they want to make quick money." As we all know that everything has pros and cons same is the case with crypto airdrop. Still, we should not feel in this discussion of good or bad. If you have research about it and in your view, it can be fruitful for you, do not look back just avail the opportunity and if it has negative aspects, so drag your hands out of it.

Types of Airdrops
Due to the opportunities provided by the Airdrop system, so many airdrop types have been introduced in the market, offering different specifications. Some of the types are as follow;

Standard Airdrop
A standard cryptocurrency airdrop transfers an amount of native coin or token into existing wallets as a

marketing strategy. It is usually to promote the brand and encourage more people to adopt the asset, often during their initial coin offering.

Generally, all you need to do is sign up for an account with the new project, and provide your wallet address during the distribution event.

Bounty Airdrop

Bounty airdrops are also a marketing strategy, but potential recipients have to engage in some promotional activity to receive the digital asset.

These activities could include:

Sharing a post about the blockchain project on Twitter or other social media platforms;

Signing up for the project's email newsletter;

Joining a forum to discuss and participate in the project;

It takes a bit more work to get a free token through a bounty airdrop than a standard airdrop, but the activities usually aren't demanding.

Exclusive Airdrop

An exclusive airdrop sends crypto coins out to a group

of people who follow an airdrop aggregator. These third-party sites share news about promising crypto projects and upcoming airdrop events.

Holder Airdrop
Holder airdrops go to people who have some amount of another cryptocurrency in their wallets. Usually, the crypto project takes a snapshot of crypto holdings on a specific date, then let people claim an airdrop based on their ownership at that time.

For example, Stellar is a crypto project that started in 2014. In 2016, its leaders announced a plan to airdrop $19 billion worth of lumen (XLM), its native cryptocurrency, to existing bitcoin (BTC) holders as a nod of respect to the Bitcoin network.

To receive the reward from the Stellar airdrop, you had to verify your BTC holdings to claim the XLM.

Pros and Cons of Crypto Airdrop
As we know that everything has advantages and disadvantages in their specific field same is the case with crypto airdrop. One of the prime advantages of airdrop is that it provides an opportunity for the company to promote it. But, which is a straightforward and low-cost promotion? As we all know, success in

marketing is not possible without valuable promotions, and airdrop provides that platform.

The people can hear and gain knowledge about cryptocurrency through an airdrop; the individuals can be educated about cryptocurrency and their usage and can be valuable in fundraising.

One of the main advantages is that people who don't have enough money can use this platform to make some money by promoting the cryptocurrency through airdrop and receiving free dollars in return. This airdrop strategy is well known and is very good for the newbies with less budget in their wallets. So it can be a win-win situation for both company and users if the value of money rises at some stage.

The thing that does not work in favor of airdrop is that they have to provide a very calculated amount of tokens which is indeed a hard task if they issue fewer tokens so it may result in zero marketing or if they provide a greater amount so it can pollute the market value of the tokens.

To some extent, the company might run out of token as they will provide tokens to users all over, so the shortage of tokens can occur, resulting in losses sometimes.

The other disadvantage can be that the recipients of the free tokens might sell them even before getting the status of a seller, which can devalue the tokens.

How to Discover Airdrops?

The first step in profiting from the airdrops goldmine is discovering them. You have to be a frequenter of crypto sites, such as Bitcointalk, to hear about new airdrops. Interestingly, airdrops are easier to find. This is mainly due to the emergence of dedicated airdrop websites and social media channels that track airdrops and post them daily. These aggregating sources make finding airdrops easier, and those who maintain them benefit from people using their referral links.

How Profitable Are Airdrops?

Every once in a while, an airdrop can be hugely profitable. The best example I actually know about is the story I heard about a man who gained massively from the recent airdrop of Oyster Pearl. He received over 2400 PRL, which eventually went up in value to over $5 per token. He sold just under half of his holdings. The airdrop he received of Polymath is a slightly more common, yet still not typical, result. He got 250 POLY, which has since been valued at between $90-$200. More often than not, however, the amount of tokens you get is so small it is barely worth the gas to send it to an exchange. Many tokens will also never be worth anything, either because the project wasn't severe or it just fails as a business.

How do you receive crypto airdrops?
Crypto airdrops can be a great way to add to your crypto portfolio without having to buy any assets using fiat currency.

Some ways to track down crypto airdrops are:
- Performing regular searches online for crypto airdrop opportunities
- Following airdrop aggregators and signing up for their exclusive airdrops
- Signing up for new platforms to take advantage of any standard airdrops they offer
- Monitoring up-and-coming projects to prepare for bounty airdrops

Taking advantage of an upcoming airdrop is mostly a matter of keeping up with developments and jumping on opportunities as they arise.

Airdrop Scams
As good as the airdrop sounds, you need to know that one disadvantageous thing about airdrop is there are some scams out there. Below, I describe the most

common airdrop scams I have come across and how you can avoid them. But, unfortunately, some scammers are also working in the same system. They can deceive you by sending you several bitcoins without informing or notifying you and then put their demands in front of you; if you fulfilled those demands, there is every chance they can deceive you and take your all valid and deserved money.

Dump Airdrops

Not all airdrops are focused on building value or community. In a dump airdrop, the goal for the developers is to generate short-term buzz about a token so that people will be eager to buy it when it hits exchanges. Once it does, the developers quickly sell (dump) all their tokens for a tidy profit. Once they have dumped as many as possible, they disappear, and the project becomes inactive. Arguably, this is not a straight-up scam since the token is real. However, the goal is to create a situation where the developers benefit financially from dumping tokens they have no plans to develop further.

An excellent example of a dump airdrop was EDOGE in 2017. The EDOGE developers claimed to be trying to breathe new life into Dogecoin by creating a version on the Ethereum blockchain. The project sent 5 million EDOGE to those who registered for the airdrop. The developers succeeded in creating a buzz. Yet, when the token hit exchanges, airdrop recipients discovered their tokens were locked, which meant they could not send them.

Meanwhile, hundreds of millions of EDOGE were being dumped on multiple exchanges. The strong suspicion was the developers were selling off all the tokens they had held back for themselves. The price of EDOGE quickly plummeted to a point where it became virtually worthless. The project was abandoned, and its social media accounts went dead.

It can be hard to spot a dump airdrop, but a good approach is to spend a bit of time with the project's website and whitepaper. Typically, those behind a dump airdrop will not put much time into either, and the superficiality will show through.

Private Key Scams

Private key scams are entirely fake airdrops. They are designed to trick you into giving out the private key to your wallet. A legitimate airdrop asks participants for their wallet's public address. However, a scam airdrop asks for the private key to your wallet as well. Those who don't fully understand how a crypto wallet works and how little you can trust people on the internet are most likely to fall victim to this scam.

Avoiding this scam is simple and relatively easy. First, do not give out your private key for any reason. If you are ever asked for it, be it on a form, a website, or through direct messaging, do not give it out because you are dealing with a scam. There is no reason a private key is needed for an airdrop. The only reason someone would ask for it is to steal whatever is in your wallet.

Information Trolling

Another type of scam airdrop I came across was designed to collect personal information, either to sell to third parties and/or to use for future phishing attempts. These scams claim to be giving away tokens, but the projects are fake. The goal is to get your email address, wallet address, social media info, etc. While a bit less dangerous than private key scams, these are still very risky. I participated in some earlier ones in my crypto career and noticed many phishing emails coming through my inbox.

The best way to avoid information trolling airdrop is to research the apparently behind the project. Most do not have a website, let alone a whitepaper or social media presence. If a project has no website or whitepaper, any advertising airdrop should be avoided.

Bait and Switch

I have also encountered what I like to call "bait and switch" airdrops. This scam lies in tricking you into signing up for other things, so someone else gets referral credit. Sometimes the referrals are for other airdrops. In this case, you could be asked to sign up for "partner" airdrops. The reality is these are not partners. The airdrop form is merely an intelligent way for a scammer to generate referrals. Another version of this scam asks you to sign up to a specific crypto exchange so the scammer can benefit from a referral. Yet another version I have seen tries to get you to join pump and dump groups, often on Discord or Telegram. In all these cases, the common denominator is the airdrop is fake, and the form is just a way of getting you to sign up for other things.

Bait and switch scams don't cost anything, but they are an annoying waste of time. They can also be tricky to spot because legitimate airdrops do ask you to join social media accounts or register on their website. A bait and switch airdrop will ask you to sign up for other projects, create accounts on exchanges, or join a discord or Telegram group not explicitly dedicated to the project supposedly behind the airdrop. The best way to avoid them is to not participate in any airdrop that asks you to sign up for unrelated projects or social media channels.

How to Navigate Airdrop Risks

The first thing you might need to understand is that not all airdrops are benevolent. Therefore, as a trader, you need to be very careful of which airdrops you sign up for. Firstly, if an airdrop requires you to send any funds to its project, it is almost certainly a scam. Pease do not do it.

Secondly, some airdrops are simply vehicles to get personal information from you, and "dusting" attacks are common, in which you receive a fractional amount of crypto into your wallet and thereby reveal your public address to a potential scammer or hacker. Once a project has your public address, its members can easily check your portfolio through block-chain explorer tools. So you have got to be very careful.

Suppose you are holding a valuable sum of crypto assets on that wallet address. In that case, you could theoretically get targeted through phishing, SIM swap and other hacking attempts, or real-life extortion and violence.

Therefore, it's best to create a new wallet specifically for airdrops. This is pretty simple. As most airdrops happen on the Ethereum network as ERC-20 tokens, simply set up a new address on the likes of MetaMask or My Ether Wallet to receive airdrops. This will also enable you to separate that "house money" from coins you have paid for.

Conclusion

From the above discussion, it is concluded that airdrop can be considered the hidden goldmine as it gives strength to the cryptocurrency market by promoting it in a broader range. Despite the challenges mentioned above, airdrops are fun to get into cryptocurrency and find out about new blockchain projects. Every once in a while an airdrop can also be hugely profitable.

My advice is to hold onto airdrop tokens on the chance they become valuable in the future, or at least worthy enough to sell for a decent amount of BTC or ETH during the next bull market. I would also recommend looking at the project behind an airdrop to see if it has any chance of succeeding. If the project seems genuinely hopeless, I will pass, no matter how many tokens are given away.

JOIN CRYPTO MASTERCLASS NOW

One popular quote by Steve Marabolli that I believe every man should live by is this. "While intent is the seed of manifestation, action is the water that nourishes the seed. Your actions must reflect your goals in order to achieve true success." This is actually very true.

I see so many people with good intentions but only few people take actions. As good as your intentions could be, they can't make you successful if you don't take action. One of the action I believe you have taken towards success is by acquiring this book and that alone isn't enough. You have gotten the basic knowledge simplified in a detailed form, but yet you might need guidance so you can understand more about the journey you are about to embark on.

Your first success towards financial freedom starts with your acquisition of more knowledge and getting a mentorship. Knowledge propels you on the journey but mentorship speeds it up. Knowledge is like your fuel for the car, mentorship is the nitro. Knowledge gives you speed, mentorship gives you acceleration (speed plus direction).

I see a lot of people with the desire to gain more knowledge about crypto and in 2017, I decided to create a class that teaches people how to start the cryptocurrency journey and also guide them to make the right choices in terms of making the right trading decisions and managing their risks.

The Cryptocurrency Master Class has over the years admitted, built and nurtured individuals who are experts in the cryptocurrency market and have gained financial freedom. The Cryptocurrency Masterclass is designed to bring you from knowing nothing about cryptocurrency to knowing just everything it takes to become an expert. The classes are easily relatable and the instructors which include myself are professional crypto traders who have been in the market for years.

If you will be taking your journey a little bit further, then I will advise you apply for the Cryptocurrency Master Class where you can get to learn more about the Crypto Market and also enjoy some mentorship including signals.

To enroll, **visit www.cryptomasterclass.ng**

As I always say "No Nigerian comes to cryptocurrency and wants to look back. It's a big opportunity." But I don't think that only applies to Nigerian as I have noticed over the years that no individual ever comes to the crypto market and wants to look back. It's a massive opportunity. Take hold of this opportunity and don't let it go.

To enroll, visit **www.cryptomasterclass.ng**

See you at the top!

Connect us across all social media platforms

Twitter: /connectwithtola
Facebook: /connectwithtola
Instagram /connectwithtola

Made in the USA
Middletown, DE
23 March 2022